OCD Workbook

by Laura L. Smith, PhD

for dummies®
A Wiley Brand

OCD Workbook For Dummies®

Published by: **John Wiley & Sons, Inc.,** 111 River Street, Hoboken, NJ 07030-5774, www.wiley.com

For general information on our other products and services, please contact our Customer Care Department within the U.S. at 877-762-2974, outside the U.S. at 317-572-3993, or fax 317-572-4002. For technical support, please visit https://hub.wiley.com/community/support/dummies.

Wiley publishes in a variety of print and electronic formats and by print-on-demand. Some material included with standard print versions of this book may not be included in e-books or in print-on-demand. If this book refers to media that is not included in the version you purchased, you may download this material at http://booksupport.wiley.com. For more information about Wiley products, visit www.wiley.com.

Library of Congress Control Number: 2026947687

ISBN 978-1-394-43178-6 (pbk); ISBN 978-1-394-43180-9 (ebk); ISBN 978-1-394-43179-3 (ebk)
SKY10164403_080326

Table of Contents

Introduction

Obsessive-compulsive disorder (OCD) is the fourth most common mental health condition in the world. Many people suffer from it for years, decades, or often a lifetime without ever getting help. Yet there are evidence-based treatments that work.

People with OCD are often skilled at keeping their suffering silent. They often feel deeply ashamed of their thoughts or behaviors. Some believe that no one can possibly understand and help them. Others may be too fearful to divulge their secret obsessions or compulsions, thinking that people will consider them crazy.

In my psychotherapy practice, I frequently worked with people who had been diagnosed with anxiety, depression, substance abuse, or even psychosis only to find that beneath all their suffering were unreported obsessions and compulsions. Some of these clients had been in therapy for years without getting better. After their OCD was addressed with the proper treatment, they were able to benefit from therapy and greatly reduce their suffering. Some became symptom free.

This book is for all people who struggle with OCD, their friends, family members, and the therapists that work with them. Throughout these pages I paint a clear picture of all of the aspects and faces of OCD. With greater understanding and proper treatment, you can start a path toward help and healing. I offer you exercises to complete to help you walk forward in your journey. Here there is no judgment, no rush, only kindness, and acceptance.

About This Book

OCD Workbook For Dummies describes the many symptoms of OCD, both obsessions and compulsions. Worksheets throughout the book allow you to plot your own particular obsessions and compulsions.

It also provides a comprehensive treatment plan for OCD. In clear, concise, and understandable language, the book explains how to apply evidence-based techniques in the treatment of OCD. For those with mild cases, this book can serve as a self-help tool. However, most people with OCD should consider working with a psychotherapist.

This workbook can easily be used in psychotherapy as an outline for treatment. Exercises and worksheets can be completed either as homework or during the session.

If you like, start at the beginning and work through the whole book. But you don't have to read every chapter. Feel free to skip around, dipping in and out where you find the information you need. In addition, don't worry about memorizing anything. This book is a reference, and you can use the table of contents and index to find specific topics that interest you.

Within this book, you may note that some web addresses break across two lines of text. If you're reading this book in print and want to visit one of these web pages, simply key in the web address exactly as it's noted in the text, pretending as though the line break doesn't exist. If you're reading this as an e-book, you've got it easy — just click the web address to be taken directly to the web page.

Foolish Assumptions

In writing this book, I made a few assumptions about you. In particularly, I assumed that you may:

- Think you have symptoms of OCD and want to find more information
- Have been diagnosed with OCD and are ready to find appropriate treatment
- Care about someone with OCD and want to understand how to help
- Be a mental health professional wanting to use this book as a resource during therapy with clients who have OCD
- Be a student studying OCD or psychology and want to learn more

Icons Used in This Book

Throughout this book, I use icons in the margin to flag certain kinds of information. Here's a guide to what the icons mean:

TIP

The Tip icon highlights material that may be particularly useful in your understanding and beating OCD.

WARNING

I use the Warning icon to warn you about something that may cause you an increase in symptoms or some other problem.

REMEMBER

Anything flagged with the Remember icon is important information that it's worth remembering.

TECHNICAL STUFF

Sometimes I wade into the weeds on a subject. When I do, I mark it with the Technical Stuff icon. If you're short on time or you just want the information you need, you can skip anything marked with this icon. But if you enjoy digging a bit deeper, read on.

Beyond the Book

In addition to what you're reading right now, this product also comes with a free access-anywhere Cheat Sheet that covers everything from the common types of OCD to common compulsions to tips for dealing with OCD and more. To get this Cheat Sheet, simply go to `www.dummies.com` and type **OCD Workbook For Dummies Cheat Sheet** in the Search box.

In addition, *OCD For Dummies*, 2nd Edition (Wiley), contains more detailed information about OCD. You may want to use it as a companion to this workbook.

Throughout the book there are worksheets that you may want to complete more than once. Go to `www.dummies.com/go/ocdworkbookfd` to download blank versions that you can print and use. ***Note:*** After going to the page, click "Related Resources" to access the content.

Where to Go from Here

If you're reading this book because you have OCD and you want to get help, you're in the right place. You can focus on the chapters that interest you, but I encourage you to flip around so you can get strategies from many different perspectives.

Finally, if you have OCD that interferes with living a full life, I strongly suggest that you find a professional to help you strategize and support your treatment.

1 The Ins and Outs of OCD

IN THIS PART . . .

Take a look at the components of obsessive-compulsive disorder (OCD).

Understand that obsessions can be repeated thoughts, impulses or urges.

See that compulsions give quick but temporary relief.

Recognize the mental health disorders that sometimes go along with OCD.

Check out the many possible causes of OCD.

IN THIS CHAPTER

» Finding out about OCD

» Observing obsessions

» Considering compulsions

Chapter 1

Dissecting Obsessions and Compulsions

Obsessive-compulsive disorder (OCD) is a complex set of symptoms that include obsessions and compulsions. Like most mental health conditions, symptoms can range from mild to severe. Many people with OCD live very successful lives, despite symptoms, Others are debilitated and unable to experience positive relationships or perform the tasks necessary for a productive life.

This chapter explains the basic symptoms of OCD, including obsessions and compulsions. It also describes the elements that make up the diagnosis of OCD.

TIP

If you believe that you or someone you care about has OCD, it's best to be seen by a licensed mental health provider trained in assessment and diagnosis.

Understanding Obsessive-Compulsive Disorder

In obsessive-compulsive disorder (OCD), *obsessions* are upsetting, intrusive mental events, and *compulsions* are behaviors or actions that someone does, either mentally or physically, in order to reduce the distress caused by the obsession. For example, a person may have an obsessive worry that they'll forget to turn off the stove and burn the house down; the compulsion is checking the stove over and over to make sure that the stove is really off.

There is nothing inherently wrong about being "obsessive" or "compulsive" outside the realm of OCD. For example, if you're having surgery, you most certainly want the operating room to be as germ-free as possible. That calls for a team of people who are obsessively concerned about cleanliness, including your doctors, nurses, and techs who wash their hands over and over.

Also, during surgery, there's compulsive counting. Prior to the operation, all the instruments, sponges, and gauze are counted. During the surgery, anyone involved can call a count. During that count, the whole staff stops until everything is accounted for. When the surgery is over, a final count is made. This compulsive counting has reduced the significant error of sewing someone up after surgery with a sponge or piece of equipment left inside.

These are excellent examples of medical teams being obsessive and compulsive. However, these behaviors are perfectly normal, expected, and desired. That's different from OCD, where the thoughts are intrusive and disrupt a person's daily life. OCD is a chronic mental health disorder in which people experience repetitive thoughts, images, or urges followed by a need to perform some action to decrease discomfort. These patterns occur multiple times a day and interfere with daily living.

In this section, I help you determine whether you may have OCD and differentiate what's typical from what's not.

Taking a look at the differences between worries, superstitions, and OCD

As I explain in the introduction to this section, some obsessions and compulsions are perfectly normal, so it can be hard to tell if you really have OCD. Worksheet 1-1 may give you some clues.

Count how many items you answered yes to. Was it more than one? Two? Three? I hope so. Most humans have some superstitions or weird random thoughts. In fact, occasional obsessional thinking and compulsive actions are perfectly normal.

While driving, you may have a strange thought of hitting someone with your car. While walking, you may suddenly have an image of shoving someone into traffic. Parents may have images of harming their babies. Who hasn't washed their hands excessively after picking up something gross with a paper towel? These thoughts and behaviors are common and expected when they happen once in a while. In fact, researchers have found that 90 percent of people report having a few superstitions and obsessional thoughts, images, or impulses.

TIP

Although the content of OCD obsessions and compulsions can seem normal, the difference between everyday bizarre or superstitious thinking and OCD is the frequency, duration, and suffering these thoughts or images produce. Someone with OCD is stuck in an almost constant loop of obsessions and compulsions. And their misery and anguish are quite intense.

WORKSHEET 1-1 Reasonable or Irrational?

Yes	No	Have you ever . . .
		Felt like you might be contaminated by being in a hospital?
		Counted the steps most of the time you walked up the stairs?
		Felt sure you made a mistake and repeatedly rechecked completed work?
		Had a headache and worried it was a brain tumor?
		Worried about bad luck after cracking a mirror?
		Rechecked the locks in your house?
		Had a sudden urge to drive off the road?
		Felt an intense need to clean your house?
		Felt a strong need to repeat things a certain number of times?
		Unexpectedly wondered about your real sexual orientation?
		Worried you might blurt out something grossly inappropriate?
		Got out of an elevator on the 13th floor and felt uncomfortable?
		Spent too much time arranging your cupboards?
		Avoided stepping on cracks in the sidewalk?
		Felt like washing your hands excessively?
		Had an image that you might hurt someone you care about?
		Believed that bad things always come in threes?
		Repeated certain prayers multiple times a day?
		Had a weird sexually deviant thought run through your mind?

Checking out symptoms

My brother arranges his spices in alphabetical order. In fact, they're all the same size and brand and spaced pretty much 1/4 inch apart in his cupboard. Does he have OCD? He's obviously pretty obsessive about the arrangement, and he'd probably compulsively rearrange them if someone in his kitchen messed them up. But he doesn't spend a lot of time looking at his spices, or thinking about his spices, or checking to make sure that they remain in the correct order. He has other interests, and his spice arrangement doesn't make him miserable.

OCD involves uncontrollable and frequent obsessive thoughts, images, and impulses that bother you. People with OCD feel driven to compulsively react to those obsessions. If my brother had OCD, he would spend hours thinking about his spices and worry constantly that they somehow had gotten out of order. He'd likely compulsively take the spices out of the cupboard and rearrange them to somehow quell the painful doubt. The obsession and compulsion would take time away from every day and get in the way of his other activities.

REMEMBER

OCD is a pattern of obsessions that lead to compulsions. The compulsions are an attempt to relieve distress. The relief following a compulsion is fleeting, and the obsessions come roaring back. This pattern is persistent over time and interferes with being able to carry out normal daily responsibilities.

TIP

In Worksheet 1-2, take some time to reflect on your symptoms — particularly those that interfere or disrupt your life in some way. For example, are you often late for appointments because you can't stop checking to make sure the door is locked? Writing helps clarify thinking. Don't worry about grammar or punctuation or writing something intelligent — just let the words flow.

WORKSHEET 1-2 My Reflections on My Symptoms

____

____

____

____

____

____

____

____

____

____

____

____

____

____

____

____

____

Diving Deep into Obsessions

Obsessions are houseguests that stay too long. They barge in, uninvited, and steal your mental space and peace. Obsessions make you feel uneasy, angry, shameful, dirty, disgusted, crazy, or afraid. Obsessions come in three forms:

» **Thoughts:** Everyone has thoughts, but obsessive thoughts are unwanted and intrusive. You may have the thought that you forgot to lock the door even though you just locked it. Or you may think that your kitchen is dirty and full of germs despite having cleaned it an hour ago. Perhaps you continuously think about not being fully prepared for work or school, even with constant positive feedback.

- **Urges:** Urges are feelings that you may not be able to control yourself and do something horrible or inappropriate. You may worry that you'll shout out something very rude and inappropriate at a work meeting. Or as you walk by someone on the street, you may have a sudden unwanted urge to push them into traffic.
- **Images:** Obsessive images are extremely distressing mental pictures, often of unwanted violent, sexual, strange, and disgusting scenes. They commonly involve your doing something you'd never do, but they pop up, unwelcome, into your mind.

Everyone has an occasional obsessive thought, urge, or image. In fact, sometimes obsessive thinking can be helpful. For example, some people become obsessive about finishing a project, playing bridge, collecting coins, or enjoying a new relationship. The obsessions found in OCD are *not* positive.

In the following sections, I describe the qualities of OCD obsessions and list some common obsessions. I also give you a chance to think through your own obsessions.

Characteristics of obsessions

OCD obsessions are fears or concerns about uncertainty. They all involve "what if" thinking. In addition, they have the following characteristics:

- **They occur frequently.** Obsessions tend to flood the mind despite attempts to avoid or suppress them. They overtake rational thinking.
- **They're uncontrollable.** When an obsession comes along, it pushes out everything else. Distraction doesn't work, and the obsession takes hold.
- **They're disconnected.** No matter what you're doing, obsessions can occur. The most riveting movie or TV show can't keep obsessive thinking away.
- **They're upsetting.** Obsessions are not benign thoughts. They're distressing, scary, and highly disruptive.

Common obsessions

There are an infinite number of possible obsessions. Unlike other mental health disorders, OCD symptoms have extreme variations. However, many contain certain clusters of fears, worries, or doubts. The most frequent of these obsessive clusters include the following:

- **Fears about being contaminated by almost anything:** These worries are usually about germs or dirt, but they can also include extra-terrestrial energy, carpet fibers, or sticky food.
- **Doubts about having done or not done something:** Often called *checking OCD,* people worry about locking the doors, turning off the stove, making mistakes, or losing someone's love or approval.
- **Needs to do or have something just right:** These obsessions usually include a need for symmetry. Sometimes called *just-right OCD,* these symptoms might involve arranging objects, having a perfect or complete collection, keeping the blinds around the house even, doing a particular act slowly or quickly or in some unusual, quirky way.

» **Superstitions or rituals that must be performed or something horrible will happen:** This may include needing to chant, count, or recite something. Or being obsessed about passing a cemetery and avoiding anything that may be related to death. Examples are endless.

» **Embarrassing, shameful, or inappropriate thoughts, urges, or impulses:** These are usually about hurting someone, doing something sexually inappropriate, shouting out obscenities, or having endless questions about the meaning of life or something else unanswerable.

» **Obsessive thoughts, impulses, and urges about the possibility of harming your child:** This form of OCD usually occurs shortly after the birth of a baby. It's appropriate for parents to worry about keeping their kids safe, but parents with this sort of OCD are overwhelmed and extremely frightened by these obsessions.

» **Obsessive feelings and sensations that demand attention:** These are usually associated with being something that is happening in the body. For example, some people become overly focused on swallowing or blinking. Some can't stand the sound of a particular voice or obsessively pay attention to the motor of the refrigerator.

REMEMBER

OCD obsessions are strong and compelling. They cause significant emotional pain and suffering. OCD obsessions invade and disrupt each and every day.

In Worksheet 1-3, reflect about your obsessions. Again, don't worry about grammar or punctuation or writing something intelligent — just get your thoughts down.

WORKSHEET 1-3 My Reflections on My Obsessions

Counting Up Compulsions

Compulsions are acts that you feel pressure to do in response to an obsession — for example, excessively washing your hands, repeatedly turning on and off lights, lining up books in a certain way, or counting out loud. A person with OCD believes that by doing the compulsive act, their obsession will be tamed. Unfortunately, the relief is insufficient and short-lived.

In the following sections, I explain what compulsions look like and what some common compulsions are. I also give you the chance to reflect on your compulsions.

Qualities of compulsions

Compulsions are intended to reduce anxiety after an obsessional worry. They temporarily reduce discomfort. They may also be in response to a specific urge, such as repeatedly washing hands after feeling dirty or contaminated.

Compulsions can also be the avoidance of something that may be viewed as harmful. For example, someone may avoid using an appliance because of fear that it may catch fire or avoid going to any public restroom because they believe that it's contaminated. A person with OCD may drive extra miles to avoid passing a cemetery or avoid handling a knife because they're worried about stabbing someone close by.

Compulsive rituals involve doing something in a certain way in response to an obsession. Someone may have to count to seven after leaving the house to prevent danger, or put on their clothes in a certain ritualistic order.

Compulsions often involve asking others for reassurance. Partners may ask for frequent reassurance that they're still loved or repeatedly ask if others are mad at them. People with health-related OCD may spend lots of time searching for various diseases that they may have and make frequent visits to their healthcare providers.

Common compulsions

Like obsessions, the variety of compulsive acts is infinite. However, they do seem to group together in some common categories:

- Chanting, ordering, or counting
- Cleaning and sanitizing
- Checking and rechecking
- Avoiding certain places, people, or objects

» Seeking reassurance

» Arranging things just right

» Repeating activities

In Worksheet 1-4, reflect about your own compulsions. As always, don't worry about grammar or punctuation — you aren't being graded.

WORKSHEET 1-4 My Reflections on My Compulsions

IN THIS CHAPTER

» Opening up about obsessions

» Coming clean about compulsions

» Summarizing severity

Chapter 2 Digging Deeper into OCD

Treating obsessive-compulsive disorder (OCD) requires a comprehensive awareness of all aspects of your obsessions and compulsions and how they impact your life. To figure that out, taking an honest look at all the possible symptoms gives you the best chance to decrease, diminish, and conquer obsessions and compulsions. This chapter helps you understand and admit to all the obsessions and compulsions that prevent you from living a life unimpeded by OCD.

Categorizing Your Obsessions

Determining the content of your obsessive thinking is the first step in treating OCD. There are many different ways to categorize OCD obsessions, but the following broad categories capture the most common obsessions. In the next sections, make a note of any that may be ones you're often bothered by.

TIP

Obsessions set off a *fight-or-flight response*, your body's response to danger. This response includes fear, anxiety, increased heart rate, tense muscles, and other automatic reactions. Those physical responses allow you to flee, fight, or freeze. People with OCD are constantly in a state of distress.

WARNING

Your OCD may try to convince you that obsessions are reasonable and normal. You may hesitate to admit that you're bothered by them. Be sure to be honest with yourself, and note that obsessional thinking is part of OCD when completing the following exercises.

There are an infinite number of possible thoughts, urges, or impulses that become OCD obsessions. The following sections list the most common ones.

Contamination and disgust

Most people are disgusted by germs or filthy bathrooms. However, people with OCD have *intense* anxiety and disgust, so much so that they worry and think about the possibility of being contaminated for hours each day. The following are relatively common contamination concerns:

- Blood
- Chemicals (toxic or household)
- Contact with contaminated places (hospitals, medical offices)
- Contact with dead animals or insects
- Contact with disabled people
- Contact with sick people
- Contaminated numbers, words, or phrases
- Contaminated thoughts
- Dirt
- Evil or the devil
- Feces
- Gases
- Germs
- Getting sick from animals (rabies, insect bites)
- Possible contamination from a smell
- Possibly contaminated food
- Poisonous plants
- Sharp objects or broken glass
- Spreading germs or contamination to others
- Sticky substances (sap, sticky food, grease)
- Sweat
- Urine

In Worksheet 2-1, take some time to reflect on whether you have any obsessions about being contaminated. As always, just let the words flow — don't worry about grammar or punctuation.

WORKSHEET 2-1 My Reflections on Obsessions: Contamination and Disgust

Checking and doubting

People with checking and doubting obsessions have excruciating worry that they've made a mistake that could have catastrophic consequences. Everyday worries become constant companions. Common checking and doubting concerns include:

- Causing bad things to happen
- Financial loss because of a careless error
- Hitting someone with your car
- Hurting someone because of carelessness
- Leaving appliances on
- Leaving doors or windows unlocked
- Leaving faucets on
- Making a mistake

In Worksheet 2-2, reflect on whether you have any obsessions surrounding checking and doubting.

WORKSHEET 2-2 My Reflections on Obsessions: Checking and Doubting

Symmetry: Just right

It's perfectly normal to enjoy an orderly desk or a neat house. But people with symmetry OCD have an excessive and intense need for perfection, exactness, balance, or alignment. And when things aren't just right, they're extremely unhappy. Here are some examples of symmetry obsessions:

- Cupboards being organized (alphabetically, by shape, by brand, and so on)
- Objects being arranged in a precise way
- Perfection in grooming
- Requiring balance
- Needing to say certain things in a special way
- Tapping or doing things in a certain way
- Needing to know everything perfectly about a certain subject
- Needing to keep things symmetrical (fringe, pillows, objects)
- Needing numbers to be in a certain order
- Needing handwriting to be a certain way

In Worksheet 2-3, reflect on whether you have any obsessions surrounding things being just right, perfect, or symmetrical.

WORKSHEET 2-3 My Reflections on Obsessions: Just Right

Shameful, embarrassing, repetitive, and inappropriate

These obsessions are particularly painful. Inappropriate impulses, urges, or thoughts grab people who afflicted by them.

REMEMBER

OCD obsessions do not represent any sort of repressed desire. You don't *want* to succumb to these urges or see these images. These thoughts haunt your mind but don't reflect any moral shortcoming.

Inappropriate urges or impulses that are sexual in nature often consist of:

- An urge to do something inappropriate with others
- Fears about forgotten inappropriate sexual acts

- Mental images of others having sex
- Perverse or forbidden sexual thoughts
- Thoughts of being a different sexual orientation than you are
- Thoughts of being unable to control sexual impulses
- Thoughts of having sex with animals
- Thoughts of having sex with children
- Thoughts of having sex with family members
- Thoughts of having sex with strangers or celebrities
- Visions of clothed people naked

Themes of aggression can be thoughts, impulses, or urges to do something completely out of character. These obsessions include the following:

- Fear of pushing someone down the stairs
- Fear of shouting out obscenities in public
- Mental images of stabbing or shooting someone
- Thoughts of driving into a crowd
- Thoughts of hurting animals
- Thoughts of losing control and acting aggressively
- Thoughts of stealing or cheating

People who have OCD with sacrilegious obsessions are usually religious themselves, which makes these strange thoughts even more upsetting. Superstitions that are broken feel dangerous. Some typical obsessions include the following:

- Believing that you're possessed
- Confessing sins that haven't occurred
- Fear of having bad luck
- Fear of sinning
- Fear of unlucky numbers, letters, or words
- Fear of yelling out obscenities in a religious service
- Giving special significance to things related to death
- Having thoughts and images that seem immoral
- Having intrusive inappropriate images of a religious figure
- Overwhelming adherence to right and wrong
- Worry about being religious enough
- Worry about praying "correctly"

Many obsessive thoughts are more difficult to categorize. However, like all obsessions, they're frequent, disturbing, and uncontrollable. Some common ones concern:

- An urge to memorize useless information such as license plate numbers, slogans, or facts about famous people
- Concerns about making unlikely mistakes
- Extreme obsessive thinking about making decisions
- Fear of losing something important
- Fears about possibly breaking the law
- Superstitious thoughts about random words or images
- Wonders about the meaning of life
- Worries about speaking something in a certain way

In Worksheet 2-4, reflect on whether you have any obsessions surrounding shameful, embarrassing, repetitive, or inappropriate possible actions or behaviors.

WORKSHEET 2-4 My Reflections on Obsessions: Shameful, Embarrassing, Repetitive, and Inappropriate Behaviors

Obsessions about the body and health

People with health-related OCD have obsessive thoughts about getting sick in the future. Their obsessions may include one or more of the following:

- Belief that getting too close to people will cause illness
- Concerns that you caused someone's illness
- Expecting to die soon
- Extreme concern about an imagined defect of the body
- Extreme fear of impending death
- Fear of vomiting, urinating, or defecating in public
- Fear that others always notice a perceived imperfection
- Fear that skin changes are cancer
- Fear that suffering will be extreme
- Intense worry about mild body symptoms
- Persistent obsessions about being too fat or too thin
- Worry that their hair may be slightly out of place

TECHNICAL STUFF

There is a strong overlap between OCD health anxiety and hypochondriasis. People with *hypochondriasis* believe that they're almost always ill despite lack of medical evidence. The main difference is that, with OCD, obsessions are intrusive and incontrollable. Usually, people with OCD have some insight into the inaccuracy of their obsessions, whereas people with hypochondriasis believe that they actually *do* have an illness.

Similarly, body dysmorphic disorder and body image obsessions are very similar. People with both of these conditions believe that they have a horrible defect that causes them great distress. But the difference is that the OCD obsessions are more uncontrollable and frequent, and the person with OCD has some awareness that the perceived defect isn't really that bad, whereas a person with body dysmorphic disorder believes they really *are* that fat or thin.

In Worksheet 2-5, reflect on whether you have any obsessions surrounding your body, appearance, or current or future health problems.

Relationship and parenting obsessions

This type of OCD usually occurs when someone has obsessions about a romantic partner or a family member. But it can also involve relationships with friends, workmates, famous people, strangers, or even pets. These constant doubts can be totally false yet incredibly disruptive to both the person with OCD and their targeted relationship.

WORKSHEET 2-5 My Reflections on Obsessions: Body and Health

Intense, intrusive, disturbing obsessions often include:

- A need to know where the person is all the time
- Belief that someone you don't know has a special relationship to you
- Belief that you're incapable of love
- Constant need for reassurance of love
- Constant need to be in control of someone else
- Distress about the possibility of falling out of love
- Extreme jealousy despite lack of any reason
- Extreme worry about someone's health despite no evidence of illness
- Fear that the partnership is somehow flawed
- Strong, overwhelming concern about safety
- Thoughts you might harm your child
- Unwarranted fear of being cheated on
- Worry about being deserted

REMEMBER

All parents worry about possible harm to their children, especially parents of newborns. Parenting OCD is a state of constant obsessional tension and can interfere with bonding with and raising healthy children. If you believe you may have this type of OCD, talk with your healthcare provider for evaluation.

In Worksheet 2-6, reflect on whether you have any obsessions about relationships and parenting.

WORKSHEET 2-6 **My Reflections on Obsessions: Relationships and Parenting**

____
____
____
____
____
____
____
____
____
____
____
____
____
____
____
____
____

Obsessive concerns about feelings and sensations

Have you ever tried to go to sleep and noticed the sound or sensation of your heart beating? Not in a mindful, relaxing way, but as an annoyance that interferes with gliding off to sleep. People with OCD related to body sensations may pay obsessive attention to:

- A need to burp
- Background noises
- Blinking

» Body position (hand placement, standing certain ways, sitting correctly)
» Certain smells that are not related to contamination fears
» Heart rate or pulse
» Other people talking (sometimes one particular person)
» Repetitive music or words
» Ringing in the ears
» Specific colors
» Swallowing
» Yawning

In Worksheet 2-7, reflect on whether you have any obsessions about sights, sounds, or feelings in your body.

WORKSHEET 2-7 **My Reflections on Obsessions: Feelings and Sensations**

Considering Compulsions

Compulsions are behaviors made in response to an obsessive thought, urge, or image. For example, someone with an obsession about having perfectly arranged canned goods may feel compelled to check on their cupboards and rearrange cans in perfect order multiple times a day. These responses consume considerable time. Their purpose is to somehow relieve, protect, or remedy obsessional thoughts or beliefs. However, any relief is short-lived.

TIP

Not all compulsions are related in a logical way to the obsession. For example, someone with an obsessional fear of shouting out obscenities in church may compulsively clean their refrigerator, somehow believing that that will prevent them from shouting uncontrollably. The OCD mind is hard to understand.

All compulsions are actions (which can include having specific thoughts). Some, like handwashing, are observable. Checking that doors are locked, the stove is turned off, or items on the bedstand are correctly ordered are also overt compulsions. Many overt compulsions involve saying things out loud, such as chanting, praying, or asking for reassurance.

Other compulsions are less observable. These internal compulsions are completed in the mind. *Covert* (internal) compulsions can be any pattern of thinking imaginable. Some people may have to organize words alphabetically, repeat a word, or perhaps say things to themselves a certain number of times. Covert compulsions are also demanding, time-consuming, and do little to banish the distress of obsessional thoughts, urges, or impulses.

REMEMBER

There are an infinite number of possible compulsions. The following lists are generally considered to be somewhat typical. However, you may not find your compulsions included. That's okay — this list will help you understand and identify your own compulsion.

TIP

The American Psychiatric Association publishes a *Diagnostic and Statistical Manual of Mental Disorders* that describes the criteria for OCD. One of the specifiers includes that obsessions and compulsions take more than one hour of time per day.

Reassurance-seeking

Asking others for reassurance is a common compulsion that is a response to many of the possible obsessions. For example, someone with a contamination obsession may not only clean compulsively but also ask others if things are "clean enough."

TIP

Those seeking reassurance compulsively ask the same questions of others multiple times and still aren't sure. This compulsion comes from the need for certainty.

Here are some common reassurance-seeking compulsions:

- Are those books crooked?
- Are we going to be on time?
- Are you mad at me for something?

- Are you still attracted to me?
- Are you sure you locked the door?
- Did I do that right?
- Do you see any dust on the floor?
- Do you still love me?
- Do you think I may have hit someone with the car?
- Do you think my hair looks okay?
- Does the house smell like gas?
- Will we have enough money, food, water, gas, and so on?

All these questions are perfectly normal for someone to ask occasionally. But compulsions are never satisfied. Friends, family, and colleagues can become quite irritated by the continued questioning and reassurance-seeking behaviors.

Cleaning and decontamination

I recently sold my house. In the process, I had multiple open houses. Before each open house, I would clean. It's not that the house started out very dirty — I'm not one to leave clothes lying around or dishes in the sink. Still, it took more than two hours of polishing the faucets, making sure there were no fingerprints on the light switches, vacuuming, and straightening cushions and pillows on the couches, and then going through each room, turning on the lights, and checking to make sure it was completely clean.

I can't imagine doing that every day. But someone with an obsessional thought that having a dirty house could contaminate them in some way may regularly clean for at least two hours a day. They're pushed by their obsessional and overwhelming anxiety to compulsively clean.

Here are examples of compulsions related to contamination obsessions:

- Cleaning any areas of the home excessively
- Cleaning or changing clothes that aren't dirty
- Excessive or ritualized bathing
- Excessive or ritualized handwashing
- Excessively cleaning or bathing your children
- Having particular clothes-washing techniques
- Performing special rituals to decontaminate
- Repeatedly cleaning counters
- Requiring people entering your home to disinfect
- Ritualized grooming
- Throwing away clothes that may be contaminated

» Using special cleaning supplies

» Wearing protective clothing when not necessary

Compulsive avoidance is also a common way to deal with obsessions about contamination. These may include avoiding the following:

» Any outside activities that may be contaminated

» Certain foods

» Doorknobs

» Garbage

» Hospitals or health centers

» Money

» Particular places in the home

» Public restrooms

In Worksheet 2-8, reflect on whether you have any compulsions surrounding cleanliness or contamination.

WORKSHEET 2-8 My Reflections on Compulsions: Cleaning and Decontamination

Checking

Checking compulsions usually involve attempting to protect or prevent harm. Repeated compulsions can include such things as:

- Checking an aspect of your body such as your pulse, blood pressure, or skin for possible health problems
- Checking that appliances are turned off
- Doing something repeatedly in order to make sure that you didn't make an error
- Going back and checking that you didn't harm someone else
- Repeatedly checking that doors or windows are locked or the security system is working and on

In Worksheet 2-9, reflect on whether you have any compulsions surrounding checking.

WORKSHEET 2-9 My Reflections on Compulsions: Checking

Rituals: Arranging, repeating, counting, touching, and speed

OCD compulsions often include putting things in a certain order; repeating phrases, words, or prayers; counting objects; or touching things in a particular way. These often have little connection to the obsession that begins the sequence. For instance, someone with a contamination fear may have a compulsion to repeat the alphabet. Here are a few of the many examples:

- Arranging items in a particular order (by size, alphabetically, by color, or by position, such as 1 inch apart)
- Completing tasks either slowly or with a certain time frame that feels enough
- Counting stairs, tiles, or cars going by
- Counting to 100 when a bad thought enters the mind
- Going through doorways in a certain way or repeating until it feels just right
- Having to repeat thoughts, words, events, or actions a certain number of times
- Making things exactly symmetrical
- Needing to groom in a certain ritualized manner
- Repeating a prayer six times
- Repeating words or parts of words that others say to you
- Touching items in a pattern

REMEMBER

Although compulsions sometimes sound a bit silly, they're strong drives that a person feels are absolutely necessary to carry out. They take up time and interfere with happiness.

In Worksheet 2-10, reflect on whether you have any compulsions surrounding arranging, repeating, counting, touching, or speed.

Body and health

Obsessions related to health concerns or possible body defects usually lead to various compulsions that involve checking or asking for reassurance. Here are a few common compulsions:

- Asking others for reassurance about the correctness of your appearance
- Checking the body for symmetry, such as parting the hair in exactly the correct way or making sure that muscles are even
- Demanding repeated medical tests
- Repeatedly checking the body for possible physical symptoms such as skin changes
- Spending hours scrolling the internet to check symptoms

In Worksheet 2-11, reflect on whether you have any compulsions surrounding health concerns or body issues.

WORKSHEET 2-10 My Reflections on Compulsions: Arranging, Repeating, Counting, Touching, and Speed

WORKSHEET 2-11 My Reflections on Compulsions: Body and Health

Summarizing the Severity of Your Obsessions and Compulsions

All people have occasional obsessive thoughts and compulsive actions. Sometimes they seem out of control. However, you can ask yourself some questions about your obsessions and compulsions to see if you're likely to have OCD or to get a grasp of how severe your OCD is.

Worksheets 2-12 through 2-15 help you summarize the severity of your obsessions and compulsions so you can get a big-picture view of how OCD is impacting your life.

WARNING

Only a trained mental health professional can diagnose OCD. However, the more moderate, severe, and extreme answers you have, the more likely it is that you need professional help. Turn to Chapter 7 for treatment options.

Review the chapter and, in Worksheet 2-16, write down all your obsessions and compulsions. Then think about the severity of each by reviewing Worksheets 2-12 through 2-15. Reflect on which ones appear to be the most disturbing and bothersome. What other insights have you gained?

WORKSHEET 2-12 How Much Distress Do Your Obsessions and Compulsions Cause You to Feel?

Circle Your Severity	Describe or Comment
Mild: They're usually manageable.	
Moderate: I feel bothered and anxious quite a bit.	
Severe: They're horrible and distressing.	
Extreme: I can hardly handle them.	

WORKSHEET 2-13 How Much Time Each Day Do You Have Obsessive Thoughts and Compulsive Behaviors?

Circle Your Severity	Describe or Comment
Mild: It's usually just a few minutes during the day.	
Moderate: Some days are okay, but other days they consume more than an hour or two.	
Severe: They occur every day and take up more than two hours a day.	
Extreme: Even on my good days, my obsessions and compulsions consume most of my time.	

WORKSHEET 2-14 Can You Stop Your Obsessions or Compulsions When You Want To?

Circle Your Severity	Describe or Comment
Mild: Yes, I can distract myself.	
Moderate: Occasionally, if I'm doing something very interesting, I can control them for a bit.	
Severe: Only once and awhile, but usually I have little control.	
Extreme: I have no control over my obsessional thinking.	

WORKSHEET 2-15 How Much Do Your Obsessions and Compulsions Interfere with Your Everyday Life?

Circle Your Severity	Describe or Comment
Mild: I can do what I need to do despite my obsessions and compulsions.	
Moderate: People around me notice, and I can't get myself to do certain things, but I usually get by.	
Severe: My obsessions and compulsions keep me from having normal relationships and a good job, and they even interfere with my eating.	
Extreme: I can barely make myself get out of the house. I feel like a prisoner.	

WORKSHEET 2-16 My Reflections on My Obsessions and Compulsions

IN THIS CHAPTER

» Recognizing other mental health disorders

» Investigating the relatives of OCD

» Differentiating OCD from similar symptoms

Chapter 3
Taking a Look at the Associates of OCD

Obsessive-compulsive disorder (OCD) makes people stressed out and anxious. It's almost always chronic, and it gets in the way of everyday functioning. No wonder many people with OCD struggle with other mental health conditions.

In addition, other mental health disorders appear to be related to OCD. These conditions sometimes have similar obsessions and compulsions, but there are subtle differences. In this chapter, I describe the mental health conditions that often co-occur with OCD.

WARNING

Short quizzes help you identify whether you have symptoms of other mental health disorders. However, you should never diagnose yourself, even though it's tempting. Only a licensed healthcare provider has the perspective and training for diagnosis. If you're concerned, please talk to your healthcare provider for an appropriate referral.

Common Mental Health Issues That Tag Along with OCD

OCD increases the risk of anxiety disorders, depressive disorders, and substance abuse. Unrelenting stress and worry contribute to anxiety disorders. The hopelessness caused by unrelenting symptoms leads to depression. Substance abuse may start as an attempt to decrease the power of OCD through self-medication.

Anxiety disorders

Anxiety and worry are part of OCD. However, an additional anxiety disorder often accompanies OCD. The most common is known as *generalized anxiety disorder*, and it involves constant tension and worry about almost everything. This worry is present most of the time and interferes with happiness and daily functioning. The following are common symptoms of anxiety; check off those that you believe that you may have:

- ❑ Constant tension or feeling on edge
- ❑ Worries about the future and feelings of dread
- ❑ Irritability
- ❑ Trouble relaxing
- ❑ Fear of objects, people, and situations
- ❑ Difficulty falling asleep and staying asleep because of fear-based thoughts
- ❑ Muscle tension or gastrointestinal upset
- ❑ Not being able to control or quiet worry

If you have several of these symptoms and they bother you more than occasionally, you may have a problem with anxiety. Please consult your healthcare provider for more information.

TIP

Anxiety is a normal reaction to stressful situations. If you're anxious before a big interview, during a test, when someone you care about is sick, or when actual bad things are happening, that's not a disorder.

Depressive disorders

Unrelenting stress is a major risk factor for depression. No wonder people with OCD are more susceptible. The following symptoms are consistent with depression; check off the ones that have been bothering you:

- ❑ Sad mood for more than a few days
- ❑ Problems sleeping (too little or too much)
- ❑ Appetite changes (either having little to no appetite or being ravenous)
- ❑ Lack of interest or pleasure
- ❑ Feeling hopeless
- ❑ Lack of energy
- ❑ Feeling worthless

- ❑ Problems staying focused
- ❑ Changes in movements (slowing down or getting fidgety)
- ❑ Thoughts of harming yourself or suicidal thoughts

If you have more than a few of these symptoms and they're occurring regularly, please see your healthcare professional for an evaluation.

WARNING

If you have thoughts about committing suicide you need to be evaluated by a mental health professional right away. Make sure that you don't have any firearms in your home. Please call 988, which is the Suicide & Crisis Lifeline. The call is free. It's staffed 24/7 by compassionate, trained counselors who can talk to you and direct you to care. If your plan is imminent, call 911 or go to the hospital emergency room.

Substance abuse

People with mental health issues often turn to substances to quell the discomfort of anxiety, depression, obsessions, or compulsions. However, the quest for temporary relief of distress over time, can easily lead to addiction.

CAGE is an assessment tool used to quickly assess problem drinking. It has only four questions. CAGE stands for:

- **Cut down:** Have you ever felt like you should cut down on your drinking or drug use?
- **Annoyed:** Have people annoyed you by criticizing your drinking or drug use?
- **Guilty:** Have you ever felt bad or guilty about your drinking or drug use?
- **Eye-opener:** Have you ever had a drink or used drugs first thing in the morning to steady your nerves or get rid of a hangover?

Each yes equals 1 point; the cutoff is usually 2 points. This tool can be used for other substances as well. Having a score of 2 or more most likely indicates that you have a problem with alcohol or drug use. However, there are many more factors to consider.

WARNING

Please don't be tempted to make a self-diagnosis. Trained mental health or substance abuse counselors can help you sort out any symptoms and come up with a treatment plan if you do have problems with alcohol or other substances.

In Worksheet 3-1, take a moment to reflect on your own struggles with anxiety, depression, or substance abuse. Get a further assessment from a professional if your symptoms are interfering with your happiness or life.

WORKSHEET 3-1 My Reflections on Anxiety, Depression, and Substance Abuse

Close Ties to OCD

Have you ever behaved impulsively without thinking? Of course, everyone does from time to time. Impulsivity is what happens when you have an urge and you succumb to that urge without thinking about the future consequences. Most acts of impulsiveness are relatively harmless.

However, people with certain mental health disorders have urges that are so strong, they lead to significantly impaired functioning and misery. They experience a craving so powerful that it leads to behaviors that can cause considerable harm. These disorders are thought to share some common biological and genetic roots. Turn to Chapter 4 for a discussion of the biological features of OCD.

TECHNICAL STUFF

Impulsions and compulsions both result in some sort of behavior. The difference can be found in motivation. Impulsive behavior is usually done to provide relief or pleasure and is spontaneous — it just happens. Compulsive behaviors are actions that someone feels like they *have* to do — they're driven by a need to relieve discomfort.

Body dysmorphic disorder

Body dysmorphic disorder (BDD) is a mental health condition in which someone becomes obsessively concerned about a perceived flaw in their appearance. This leads to compulsive checking in the mirror, elaborate camouflage attempts, and even plastic surgery. People with BDD are truly miserable about what they see as a defect.

This is different from OCD because people with BDD go to extreme lengths to correct their perceived flaws, such as undergoing plastic surgery.

WARNING

BDD is a serious condition and can result in isolation, depression, and even suicide attempts. If you or someone you care about has symptoms, please get help from a mental health provider.

Skin picking: Excoriation disorder

Have you ever had a scab that you had an urge to pick at or a bit of dry skin that you wanted to scrape off? That's common human behavior. Excoriation disorder involves intense urges to pick, scratch, dig, or rub perceived skin imperfections. This excessive behavior leads to bleeding, inflammation, infections, and scarring.

People with this problem may pick for over an hour at a time, often seeming to be in a trance-like state. This condition can cause severe impairment, shame, social avoidance, and embarrassment.

Hair pulling: Trichotillomania

In this mental health condition, a person experiences an urge to pull out their own hair. Although usually on the scalp, it can also involve eyebrows, eyelashes, arm hair, leg hair, and pubic hair. There is a brief sense of pleasurable relief after pulling, but then the cycle resumes. Obvious hair loss is common among those with this problem.

TECHNICAL STUFF

The main difference between trichotillomania and OCD is that the compulsive behavior (hair pulling) provides pleasure for those with trichotillomania. In OCD, compulsions are performed to decrease anxiety.

Hoarding

Many people like to collect things. People have extensive collections of coins, stamps, figurines, or even cars. And lots of people have overstuffed garages full or rarely used tools, sporting goods, or other unnecessary objects.

Hoarders accumulate so much stuff that their homes become almost uninhabitable. People with hoarding disorder believe that they cannot discard trivial items such as junk mail, newspapers, animals, containers, clothing, food, household items, and so on. They have a need to collect and believe that there may be some future use for the things they save.

Hoarders rarely seek help because they don't believe that they have a problem. In the past, hoarding was considered part of OCD. However, the main difference is that, unlike those with OCD, hoarders are usually quite content and don't suffer emotional discomfort.

TECHNICAL STUFF

Hoarding disorders are very difficult to treat. Most hoarders think that their hoarding is totally fine and fiercely resist anyone bothering their stuff. Hoarders often come to mental health therapists because their family members or friends are so distraught by the condition of their homes. Unfortunately, forced cleanups rarely work.

Tic disorders

Tic disorders involve sudden uncontrollable urges followed by sounds or movements. Throat clearing, swearing, snorting, yelling out words, barking, repeating others' words, burping, tongue clicks, or grunting are typical verbal tics. Motor tics may involve blinking, touching things, stomping, hand gestures, facial twitches, muscle tensing, or jerky movements.

Tic disorders are responses to a biological or body urge rather than an obsessive thought. Although compulsive behaviors can appear to be similar, those with tics don't have intrusive obsessive thoughts the way people with OCD do.

TECHNICAL STUFF

Tourette's syndrome is diagnosed when someone with a tic disorder has multiple motor tics and at least one vocal tic.

Somatic symptom disorder

Somatic symptom disorder was formerly called *hypochondriasis*. People with this disorder interpret mild body sensations as evidence of a disease. They make repeated medical appointments and often change medical providers when they don't get the diagnosis and treatment they believe they need.

The difference between OCD body concerns is that people with OCD usually feel compelled to notice symptoms but have some insight that they're being unrealistic. Those with somatic symptom disorder genuinely believe that they're sick.

Eating disorders

People with eating disorders have severe disturbances in their eating, either eating too much or too little. They're overly concerned with their weight, appearance, and controlling their food intake. Eating disorders generally begin in adolescence or early adulthood and are more common in women.

People with eating disorders may engage in lying about what they eat, purging after meals, exercising excessively to lose weight, or taking laxatives. They may be extremely unhealthy due to their food intake and responses (such as vomiting) to control their weight.

WARNING

Eating disorders are serious mental health illnesses that can result in multiple hospitalizations, bone loss, brain damage, and even death. If you or someone you care about has symptoms of an eating disorder, it is imperative to have a complete physical and mental health evaluation.

People with OCD may also have concerns about food or their appearance. They may engage in restrictive eating, eat in a particular way, or feel disgust about certain foods. Although there are some similar symptoms, those with OCD usually have a more specific pattern of obsessive thinking and compulsive behaviors, frequently related to contamination or harm rather than body image.

Olfactory reference disorder

People with olfactory reference disorder believe that they smell disgusting. They believe they're so disgusting that others around them notice and are also disgusted. This belief isn't just the fleeting realization after working out at the gym that you probably stink. It's a constant, consuming belief.

Those who suffer go to extreme lengths to decrease their smell. They may shower compulsively and frequently, or use excessive deodorant or strong perfume. Some even resort to surgery to remove their sweat glands.

People with olfactory reference disorder don't consider themselves to have a mental health problem. Therefore, they don't seek treatment and haven't been studied. Thus, the relationship between olfactory reference disorder and OCD is only speculative based on a similar pattern of obsessions and compulsions.

Other impulse control disorders

Other mental health conditions involve the ability or inability to control impulses. They're similar in that they involve a tension or urge, followed by an act, followed by a sense of relief or pleasure. Some of those conditions include:

- **Kleptomania:** Uncontrolled urges to steal followed by pleasure after the act
- **Compulsive buying:** Being unable to resist buying unnecessary things — lots of unnecessary things — followed by satisfaction
- **Pyromania:** Obsession with and urges to set fires, followed by relief of tension or pleasure
- **Gambling:** Poor ability to stop gambling despite financial costs; an almost delusional belief about the next big win
- **Conduct disorders:** A pattern of defiance, opposition, aggression, and sometimes illegal behaviors despite negative consequences
- **Paraphilias:** Sexually deviant behaviors such as exhibitionism, pedophilia, fetishism, and *frotteurism* (touching or rubbing against a non-consenting person to become sexually aroused)

TIP

The ability to stop and think before acting is a critical ability for optimal functioning. People with good impulse control tend to have better educational success, financial outcomes, relationships, and even better health. Lack of impulse control, which is an underlying symptom of many of these OCD-related disorders, leads to negative outcomes across many categories.

If you have symptoms of any of the OCD-related disorders, take a moment to write them down and think about the effect they have on your life in Worksheet 3-2.

WORKSHEET 3-2 My Reflections on Disorders Related to OCD

Distinguishing among OCD Traits, OCPD, and OCD

Lots of people have obsessions and compulsions, but few people have diagnosable OCD. Here are the differences:

- ***OCD traits* are just habits that some people have.** For example, some people may count stairs every time they climb them. Others arrange their books in a particular way, maybe by color. Some people obsess about their finances, checking their accounts every day. Others are excessively clean. Do these activities cause distress? No. Do they interfere with life? Probably not.

» ***Obsessive compulsive personality disorder*** **(OCPD) is a pervasive way of living that causes problems, especially with relationships.** However, if you ask someone with OCPD whether they have a problem, they'll certainly say no.

People with OCPD are controlling, are perfectionistic, think they know everything, need excessive order, are dedicated to work, and see recreation as serious. They tend to be excessively rule-bound and frugal. People with OCPD do not suffer emotionally, except when they don't get their way. And their response is usually anger.

REMEMBER

» **OCD is a mental health disorder that involves repetitive obsessions followed by compulsions to reduce the distress of the obsessions.** OCD involves significant emotional discomfort, interferes with life, and takes considerable time every day.

If you think you have OCD traits, personality disorder, or OCD, reflect on that in Worksheet 3-3.

WORKSHEET 3-3 My Reflections on OCD Traits, OCPD, and OCD

WARNING

It's okay to speculate about and reflect on your symptoms, but don't neglect to get professional help if you're suffering.

IN THIS CHAPTER

» Taking a look at the biological causes

» Seeing family influence

» Looking for online inspirations

Chapter 4 Sifting through the Causes of OCD

If you were unlucky enough to have been born during the Middle Ages and had obsessive-compulsive disorder (OCD), you may have been locked up, tortured, killed, or exorcised. That's because, during those times, people believed mental illness was really demonic possession.

Later, OCD was blamed on deep-seated sexual drives, poor potty training, or trauma, thanks to Sigmund Freud. But now we know that OCD is not caused by the devil or some weird emotional trauma.

OCD is caused by a combination of biology and learning. But relationships are complex and there is still much that's not known. This chapter is a brief dive into current thinking about the causes of OCD.

Getting Inside Your Head: Biological Risk Factors

Every thought, whether rational or not, is generated in the brain. Every action you take, whether it's compulsive or logical, also begins with the brain. So, OCD obsessions and compulsions begin with activity in the brain. However, it isn't a simple one-way street.

Several biological factors have been linked to an increased risk for OCD. They include genetic predispositions, differences in the way parts of the brain interact with each other, and brain chemistry.

Families and OCD

Simply put, if you have someone in your family with OCD, your risk of developing the disease increases. There appears to be a genetic risk for developing OCD in some families. However, at this time, there is no specific gene related to OCD. Like many things, it appears that genes are turned on and off by other factors such as health, learning, stress, trauma, and sometimes age.

Therefore, someone with a genetic predisposition for OCD may not exhibit symptoms until young adulthood. Or infection may increase the likelihood for OCD in those genetically vulnerable. For more information, see "Infection and OCD," later in this chapter.

Interestingly, there may be an adult in your family who has obsessions about becoming contaminated by signals sent from outer space and compulsively wears aluminum foil hats. And your OCD takes the form of obsessions about keeping your home safe and compulsively checking the doors and locks multiple times a day.

Do you have any relatives with OCD? If you're not sure, ask some of your family members. Describe their symptoms and your relationship in Worksheet 4-1.

WORKSHEET 4-1 My Reflections

Brain structures and functions and OCD

The structures of the brain appear to be different in many people with OCD than those without OCD. Scientists don't know if those differences were always present or were caused by OCD. Sometimes injury to these brain areas can cause OCD-like symptoms. Brain surgery, in certain cases, can decrease OCD symptoms. And successful treatment of OCD, either with psychotherapy or medication can change the brain structure and function.

You don't need to memorize the structures of the brain to have a basic understanding of what goes wrong in the brain when you have OCD. But four important structures appear to be involved:

- **Thalamus:** The thalamus is the part of the brain that takes in information from the outside world and relays it to other parts of the brain. It receives things that you hear, see, touch, feel, taste, and smell.
- **Amygdala:** The first part of the brain to receive information from the thalamus is the amygdala. This structure instantaneously processes information. It is especially responsive to danger and is the body's early warning system.
- **Orbital frontal cortex (OFC):** Immediately after information is sent to the amygdala, it goes to the OFC. This area of the brain takes in information and then interprets, evaluates, and generates actions based on those interpretations.
- **Basal ganglia:** The basal ganglia help to control voluntary movements. It initiates, stops, and smooths out movement (including language). It allows for flexibility in responses.

REMEMBER

The amygdala responds to threats by preparing the body to fight, flee, or freeze. Fear, anxiety, increased heart rate, sweating, and other physical symptoms are a response to obsessions that are processed by the amygdala.

For people with OCD, the thalamus is likely on overdrive, surveying the environment. The amygdala overestimates risk. The OFC doesn't do a good job of tamping down the emotional response, and the basal ganglia allows repetitive thoughts and actions to continuously loop. This creates a sort of brain lock, a rigid, repetitive, overly fearful circuit.

TIP

The brain is still mysterious, and these connections are somewhat speculative and based on brain images of small samples of subjects with OCD. Scientists are sure that OCD is a biological disease, but the exact causes are complex and not entirely known.

A brief example helps show how these brain structures may be impacted in an OCD brain.

> Bob has obsessional thoughts about the need to keep things symmetrical. He believes that he must keep his refrigerator and kitchen cupboards in a certain order or something terrible will happen. Bob notices his ketchup and barbecue sauce are in the wrong order in his refrigerator. His thalamus, always on the lookout, sends that information to his amygdala. His body immediately reacts with a fight-or-flight response. This intense reaction is caused by an over-perception of threat by the amygdala without the reasoning provided by the OFC. Instead, the cortex doesn't take in actual information from the thalamus but conjures up worries and possibilities of doubt, uncertainty, and risk.

So, Bob begins the compulsive task of taking everything out of his refrigerator and rearranging them. Only to have a lingering doubt about whether he did it correctly. The basal ganglia don't turn off these unproductive thoughts or compulsive actions. Thus, the cycle repeats itself.

Someone without OCD may still like to keep the refrigerator and cupboards in a certain order. But they don't go into a fight, flight, or freeze response. They may stop and rearrange a couple of items but then go on about their day.

Brain chemistry and OCD

Neurons are cells that communicate with each other throughout the brain. Through their communication, all thoughts and actions are generated throughout the body. Neurons communicate with each other by sending signals.

Signals in the brain are electrical impulses that release *neurotransmitters*, which are the chemical messengers of the brain. The brain chemistry of people with OCD is imbalanced. Scientists continue to lack full understanding of why that happens or how to manage it, but various medications that affect these neurotransmitters often lead to a decrease in symptoms.

Disruptions in communication lead to an overall feeling of being stuck on anxious thoughts and compelled to do actions that decrease the distress. Brain regions such as the OFC, thalamus, amygdala, and basal ganglia appear to be involved in the faulty communication circuit.

TECHNICAL STUFF

The neurotransmitters that are involved in the faulty communication circuit include:

- **Serotonin:** Helps regulate mood, wakefulness, and emotional regulation
- **Dopamine:** Regulates pleasure, learning, and motivation
- **Glutamate:** Stimulates brain activity and is involved in learning, memory, and energy
- **Gamma-aminobutyric acid (GABA):** Calms brain activity, but may make symptoms worse when the levels are low

Infection and OCD

OCD symptoms have occurred following an infection. Strep throat, especially in children and teens, produces antibodies to combat the illness. Sometimes, those antibodies get carried away and begin to attack the cells in the basal ganglia (see "Brain structures and functions and OCD," earlier in this chapter).

The response to these antibodies going too far is called *pediatric autoimmune neuropsychiatric disorders associated with streptococcal infections* (PANDAS). Symptoms occur suddenly and involve OCD-like behaviors, tics, and mood changes. Although this syndrome is usually seen in children, adults with viruses have also had similar reactions.

Family Factors: Psychological Risk Factors

OCD is primarily a biologically based mental health disorder. However, the environment also has a significant impact. Some people with a genetic predisposition may not develop OCD. Others without genetic predisposition can still develop OCD. The many factors that contribute to whether someone gets OCD are complicated and not completely known.

Environmental factors and learning in childhood shape mental health functioning well into adulthood. A child with a biological risk to develop OCD may not display symptoms with the certain kinds of upbringing. Some people who have genetic dispositions for OCD may not develop it until adulthood. And in some cases, a child with very few risk factors can develop OCD because of early experiences.

In my experience working with children who have OCD and their parents, I almost always found the parents to be well-intentioned and truly trying to be the best parents they could be. However, the best intentions can sometimes have less-than-ideal outcomes. The following section details some of the parenting practices that make kids become more likely to experience OCD symptoms.

Growing a worrier

There is absolutely no evidence that parenting, by itself, leads to OCD. However, if a child has a tendency for anxiety or OCD, some styles of parenting may make matters worse.

Modeling

Perhaps the quickest way to produce a child with OCD is the combination of passing along genes and modeling OCD. Modeling is teaching the child behaviors, emotional reactions, and attitudes through observational learning.

If a parent has OCD and teaches the child to imitate their own behaviors, OCD can be nurtured. For example, a mother who needs things to be ordered just right may require her child to display toys or books by size or color or place. She may become extremely distressed when this doesn't happen, and the child quickly learns to copy what the mother wants. Another parent with contamination OCD could model excessive cleanliness and frighten the child into mimicking them.

Too much information

Parents want to protect their children from the many dangers in the world. However, sometimes parents, without realizing it, give children too much information. Well-meaning parents may frighten their children with warnings about germs and washing their hands. It's great to encourage handwashing, but there's no need to predict dire consequences for not washing perfectly every time.

Young children should be supervised at all times. That's the responsibility of adult caregivers. Preschoolers don't need to believe that kidnappers are lurking around corners ready to snatch them. Too much information about all the potential harms they may encounter is likely to scare them instead of keeping them safe.

Perfectionism

Pushing children to be perfect is a surefire way to cause anxiety and tension. Perfection is basically impossible, so expecting perfection eventually leads to failure. When children are expected to do things perfectly, they may worry about possible mistakes and stop trying altogether.

Some children who embrace the quest for perfection may become obsessional. To relieve the distress of perfectionistic obsessions, they may engage in compulsive actions, such as repeating tasks over and over until they're just right.

Misguided thinking

My grandson told me that Santa Claus is watching everyone all the time. He said he didn't exactly know how he did it, but he was sure it was happening. He's a good kid and doesn't have anything to worry about, but he looked uneasy.

I'm not trying to ban Santa, but I can see where, for certain anxious kids, especially with a perfectionistic streak, this sort of belief could be a problem. Some children who have a tendency for OCD may come to believe that if they have a bad thought, that can mean they're a bad person. And maybe Santa Claus will know!

Overprotection

Like providing too much information, overprotecting can frighten children about the actual dangerousness of the world. It's the job of parents to keep their kids safe. But overprotective parents also give the message that only they can do the protection.

That overprotection leaves kids feeling incapable of navigating everyday life on their own. They're left overestimating threats and feeling vulnerable. Their world is full of danger, and they must be always on the lookout for peril.

Parental neglect or abuse and OCD

Although many adults with OCD report abuse or neglect as children, like other parenting behaviors, it doesn't appear to be the only cause. Most adults who experience abuse or neglect as children don't have OCD. Therefore, it appears to be a factor that may interact with a biological tendency that makes OCD more likely and more severe.

Childhood abuse causes children to feel insecurely attached, have more difficulty managing emotions, and desire more control. Thus, those with that genetic predisposition are more likely to manifest OCD in an attempt to control their insecurity.

Do you have childhood experiences that may affect your OCD symptoms? If so, reflect on them in Worksheet 4-2.

WORKSHEET 4-2 My Reflections on My Childhood Experiences

When Bad Things Happen or Might Happen: Social Risk Factors

Although most people who have OCD develop it in childhood or adolescence, a few experience life events that lead to an emergence of OCD later in life. Major stressful events, such as a divorce, death of a loved one, job loss, childbirth, or trauma, can trigger OCD. These events combined with lack of resources are more likely to increase the severity of the response.

REMEMBER

Some people respond to life challenges with anxiety, depression, post-traumatic stress disorder (PTSD), or OCD. A larger group of the population face trauma with immediate distress but then find their way to resilience. Biological, psychological, and social factors interact in predicting the individual response.

Exposure to trauma

Traumatic events can lead to the development of OCD in vulnerable people. When something shocking, unexpected, painful, frightening, or unsettling happens, people become extremely alert and tuned in to their environment. This can increase obsessive thoughts, urges, or impulses, which then leads to compulsive actions to reduce distress.

For example, a person involved in a serious car accident on the freeway may begin to have obsessive thoughts about staying away from freeways. This may lead to compulsively avoiding freeways. That obsession will likely grow to include busy streets or streets with high speed limits. This may result in elaborate compulsions to avoid any street with a speed limit above 35 miles per hour. Obsessions and compulsions may also include ritualistic preparation of safety protocols such as checking and rechecking seat belts. That person may have previously had OCD traits, but the trauma of the car accident caused their symptoms to increase so much that they now have OCD.

WARNING

Some people develop both PTSD and OCD after a traumatic event. Unfortunately, those with both disorders often experience severe symptoms and have a harder time getting better with treatment. If you have both PTSD and OCD, it's especially important that you receive therapy from a well-trained mental health professional who is experienced in treating both conditions.

REMEMBER

OCD involves having obsessions and compulsions that significantly interfere with daily living and take up more than an hour each day.

Social media and OCD

Social media doesn't cause OCD, but it can certainly feed it. The internet tracks a person's browsing and search history and floods them with similar and related social media.

Social media feeds obsessions about contamination by exaggerating risk. It dashes obsessions about perfection by posting the unreachable heights of beauty or symmetry. People with OCD can also use social media to avoid their obsessions with endless, mindless, scrolling. Social media increases uncertainty and reinforces negative predictions of the future.

Social media can also act as a method of repetitive reassurance seeking. Compulsively checking screens for certainty brings short-term relief but leads to more distress. Social media becomes part of the vicious cycle of OCD.

How has exposure to trauma or the use of social media impacted your symptoms of OCD? Reflect on your experience in Worksheet 4-3.

WORKSHEET 4-3 My Reflections on Trauma and the Use of Social Media and OCD

The Worry Cycle

OCD involves a cycle of obsessions that cause distress, followed by compulsions that offer temporary relief. This cycle is fueled by what psychologists call *negative reinforcement.* Negative reinforcement occurs when some sort of discomfort or distress is stopped by an action. That action will likely reoccur more often. For instance, your pet probably knows an annoying way to get attention. My dog sticks her head up under my arm when I'm at the computer. I feel annoyed when she does that. But she stops when I pet her. She has negatively reinforced me to do what she wants.

Pain relievers are also an example of negative reinforcement. If you have a headache, you take a pain reliever to avoid the discomfort of the headache.

Your car beeps at you until you put on your seat belt. That beeping sound negatively reinforces you to buckle up.

In the OCD cycle, the discomfort caused by the obsession is decreased temporarily by performing the compulsive action. That relief negatively reinforces the compulsion.

For example, if someone has an obsessive thought that they may have been contaminated by germs, they feel anxious and frightened. They're sure that they'll come down with some catastrophic disease. To get some relief, the compulsion takes over and they engage in extensive disinfection of their entire home. After cleaning, they feel better. But that feeling doesn't last.

Another obsession occurs. Perhaps they missed something in their cleaning ritual. Maybe there's another germ and it's spreading. The result: more anxiety and fear. This time the compulsion to clean is stronger; the cleaning is more extensive and takes more time.

Figure 4-1 illustrations of the OCD worry cycle. Reflect on your own worry cycle in Worksheet 4-4.

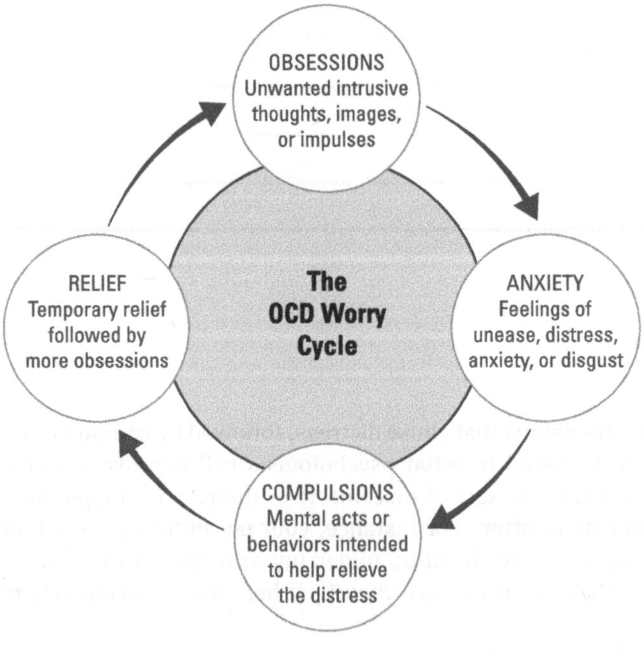

FIGURE 4-1: The OCD worry cycle.

WORKSHEET 4-4 **Worry Cycle Exercise**

What is your obsessive thought?

How do you feel? Uneasy? Anxious? Frightened?

What compulsive action do you take to help relieve your distress?

Do you feel relieved for a bit?

How long does the relief last?

Does the cycle repeat?

2

Starting Down the Treatment Trail

IN THIS PART . . .

Find out the barriers to changing obsessive-compulsive disorder (OCD).

See how the fear of change sometimes keeps you stuck.

Figure out how to battle your own obstacles.

Examine mental health providers.

Take a look at self-help options for OCD.

IN THIS CHAPTER

» Examining personal roadblocks to change

» Figuring out outside obstacles

» Reflecting on readiness

Chapter 5

Sorting through OCD Obstacles to Change

Imagine it's a beautiful hot day in the summer. You're at a swimming pool. You decide to do a cannonball off the diving board. You get to the end of the board and look down. There's no water in the pool! Lucky for you, I'm your personal psychologist, standing right behind you.

I tell you, "No worries, there's water in the pool. Jump!"

You look down. No water.

I say, "Oh, that's your OCD making you anxious. Trust me, there's water in that pool. Go ahead and do your cannonball."

Would you jump? Probably not. When people with obsessive-compulsive disorder (OCD) are faced with challenging their OCD obsessions, it's like asking them to jump into a concrete pool with no water. Their friends, family, and therapists may try to tell them they don't need to wash their hands so often, or count the ceiling tiles, or check the locks, or repeat various words. But people with OCD believe that something catastrophic will happen if they don't engage in compulsive behaviors. The immediate feeling of relief after carrying out a compulsive behavior strongly reinforces the cycle to continue.

Think about the diving board. When you resist my encouragement, turn around, and walk away from the edge of the pool, you feel a strong sense of relief. Anxiety at the possibility of jumping followed by relief when you walk away. That's how the OCD mind works.

In this chapter, you explore all the possible obstacles that keep you from getting help for your OCD. Then you identify which ones may be getting in your way.

Personal Obstacles

People with OCD suffer, but they can get better. There are evidence-based treatments for OCD, but the vast majority of people with OCD never get the care they need. In fact, statistics suggest that 80 percent to more than 90 percent of people with OCD fail to get the help they need. There are many reasons for those sad and alarming statistics. Some of them are due to the nature of OCD, which keeps many people from seeking help.

In the following sections, I describe the barriers to change. You may or may not have some or all of these challenges.

Fear of change

Doing something different or new is hard. The uncertainty of change is a normal human response. That fear interferes with treating OCD. Thoughts indicating a fear of change include the following:

- My OCD protects me from danger.
- If I work on my problems, I'll probably fail.
- I'm just not ready to take this on right now.
- This is too hard for me to handle.
- What if treatment doesn't work?
- Bad things may happen if I try to change.

REMEMBER

Obsessions are thoughts, images, and urges that lead to emotional distress. Compulsions are the actions that decrease distress.

Any treatment of OCD involves breaking up that cycle. For those with OCD, asking them to give up their compulsions feels risky, scary, and even dangerous. The belief that changing means loss of control and possible horrible consequences leads to avoidance of treatment altogether. When treatment is sought out, many people with OCD drop out before making progress because of those fears.

Shame

Feelings of shame hinder treatment of OCD. Shame makes people feel that they're flawed or unworthy of treatment. People who experience shame rarely seek treatment. Their shame also causes them to withdraw from others who may offer some support.

If they seek help, they do not disclose the true nature of their obsessions. Not admitting to their obsessions prevents the therapist from treating the core problems. Taboo thoughts about violence to others, perverted sexual acts, or moral failures are especially likely to be withheld. Those with shame mistakenly believe that if they have such perverse thoughts, they must be bad people. Those with shame may think:

- That weird thought I had about hurting my baby means I'm a horrible parent.
- I had an impulse to drive into a crowd of people. I must be a monster.
- I'm not as good as other people.
- There's something really wrong with me.
- That terrible event in the news happened because I didn't pray enough.
- I'm a pervert because I had an image of someone naked.

REMEMBER

People who experience deep shame rarely seek treatment. And if they are in treatment, underreporting or withholding symptoms from a therapist makes any treatment less likely to succeed.

Avoidance

Avoidance is a strategy that temporarily decreases discomfort and distress. Like masking symptoms with drugs or alcohol, avoidance provides short-term relief but leads to long-term increases in suffering.

- If I avoid using that restroom, I won't get sick.
- I'm not going to leave my house today so I can keep safe.
- I won't attend church because I might shout out obscenities.
- If I try, others will judge me.
- If I stay focused on social media, I won't think about hurting someone I love.

The gold standard of treatment for OCD, exposure and response prevention (ERP), requires activating OCD symptoms until distress naturally decreases (see Chapters 8 and 9 for guidance on ERP). Avoidance takes away the learning opportunity embedded in ERP. Avoidance masks the symptoms and severity of OCD and interferes with treatment. Because of this, people who avoid tend to have more severe and treatment-resistant OCD.

TECHNICAL STUFF

Habituation is the core process involved in ERP for OCD. You're exposed to the feared stimulus (the obsession) without engaging in compulsions or avoidance behaviors. Because experiencing the obsession doesn't cause the feared result, over many trials, distress or fear decreases. Habituation requires multiple exposures and response preventions. Avoidance prevents habituation from occurring.

Perfectionism

The belief that something must be done perfectly is frequently an OCD compulsion. It leads to procrastination, avoidance, repetition of tasks, and intense feelings of failure. Harsh self-criticism makes anxiety and distress worse. The fear of possibly making a mistake makes treatment seem very risky. Those with perfectionistic tendencies would rather not do anything than make a mistake.

Here are some reasons they may give to avoid treatment:

- If I'm not sure that I'll be 100 percent better, I might as well not even start.
- I'm not positive that I have the correct diagnosis. What if my OCD is something else?
- I need to be under less stress and feel better about my life before I try a new treatment.
- What if I can't do it right? I can't stand to make a mistake.

Other mental health issues

If you suffer from OCD, you're likely to have other mental health issues to deal with. A large meta-analysis found that 70 percent of those with OCD struggled with depression, anxiety, substance abuse, or other disorders. (Turn to Chapter 3 for information about co-occurring disorders and OCD.)

These other issues make treatment more challenging. For example, someone with social anxiety may be extremely reluctant to engage in therapy expecting rejection or shame. A person with depression may lack motivation to engage in any activities.

WARNING

If you have multiple mental health problems, it's important to get a thorough evaluation by an experienced mental health provider trained in diagnosis and treatment planning. In some cases, especially issues like depression or substance abuse must be addressed prior to starting treatment for OCD.

What are your personal obstacles to treatments? Fear of change? Shame? Avoidance? Perfectionism? Or other mental health issues? Write about them in Worksheet 5-1.

WORKSHEET 5-1 My Reflections on My Personal Obstacles to Treatment

Outside Obstacles

Treatment of OCD is hampered by many obstacles. Those with OCD find that deciding to begin treatment takes considerable courage. Unfortunately, for those who find the right motivation and determination to seek help, there are still more external barriers to treatment.

In the following sections, I detail obstacles that may be out of your control. It's important to know which of these challenges you may face.

Lack of treatment options

Although there are effective treatments for OCD, there is a gap between the need for treatment and the availability of trained mental health professionals. Many mental health professionals lack the specialized training necessary to carry out ERP, the most effective treatment for OCD. And those who do have the training often have long waiting lists.

TIP

A mental health professional who has training in the principles of cognitive behavioral therapy (CBT) can conduct ERP by getting additional training. The International OCD Foundation (`https://iocdf.org`) has educational conferences and on-demand webinars available for professional continuing education. In addition, using a resource such as this workbook can help you work with your therapist to conduct ERP.

Inappropriate diagnosis or treatment

People with OCD often think that their obsessions and compulsions are reasonable. In addition, embarrassment often keeps people with OCD from being entirely honest when reporting their symptoms to their therapist.

Despite feeling considerable anxiety and distress, they delay treatment. As their distress increases, they may come to a therapist and report symptoms of anxiety and depression. The therapist then treats those issues instead of getting to the core problem.

Standard treatment with medication or psychotherapy is usually unsuccessful. This leads to more severe symptoms, worse outcomes, and sometimes suicidal behavior. Specialized treatment for OCD is necessary for treatment to be effective.

WARNING

On more than one occasion, I was presented with cases of young people who had been misdiagnosed with schizophrenia, a chronic, very serious mental health condition. In these cases, a more thorough evaluation found OCD symptoms. Extensive ERP cleared up what had previously been misdiagnosed as psychotic symptoms.

Financial or location obstacles

Financial obstacles include lack of insurance or lack of insurance coverage for the sessions required to treat OCD. Traditional 50-minute hours once a week may not allow enough time for the specialized treatment necessary for treating OCD.

In addition, highly trained therapists may opt out of taking insurance altogether because of low reimbursement rates and the administrative burden of collecting fees from insurance companies. Some people with severe symptoms may require intensive programs or sometimes inpatient hospitalizations. These programs are also rarely completely covered by insurance.

To make matters worse, there is a shortage of trained professionals, and many of those are located in large cities. People who live in more rural areas often lack access to care.

TIP

Fortunately, some recent studies have found that delivering ERP through telehealth is effective in reducing symptoms. This may improve the availability of therapy to people who otherwise don't have access.

TECHNICAL STUFF

ERP via telehealth may actually improve the outcome of therapy. Because the therapy can be conducted in the client's home, exposures include real-life conditions. Telehealth can also reduce cancellations, decrease travel time, and allow family involvement.

Cultural considerations

Cultures and their expressions are diverse, so it's difficult to suggest that any certain culture presents obstacles to treatment. However, within some cultures, having a mental health issue is seen to be a sign of weakness, so symptoms are hidden from others. Other cultures may believe that these struggles should be kept private among close family members and that seeking outside help exposes the family to judgment.

Some groups may misinterpret OCD as signs of someone with a spiritual curse or moral deficiency. They may turn to traditional healing methods for help. Other symptoms may seem to be excessive expressions of virtue, like cleanliness or orderliness. Additional barriers may include language differences, lack of trust in the healthcare system, discrimination, or a lack of cultural competence on the part of the provider.

Family interference

Families of people with OCD see their suffering and want to help. They often feel guilty and helpless in understanding obsessions and compulsions and want to decrease the obvious suffering of their loved one. Unfortunately, the family's good intentions are very likely to make the OCD cycle stronger. There are various strategies that families often attempt:

- **Reassurance:** Reassurance is the most common response. It may include statements like, "Don't worry, you won't get sick," "The alarm is set — no need to check it again," "Of course I still love you," or "The kitchen looks perfectly clean."
- **Engaging in OCD behaviors:** Many partners or families become active participants in the various compulsions required by the person with OCD. Homes become excessively clean and neat, cleaning routines turn into time-consuming decontamination sessions, items are arranged in a particular order, bedtime routines have structured protocols, mealtimes become treacherous, laundry must be folded in certain ways, diets are changed, and more. These behaviors are all done to help pacify the person with OCD.
- **Changing normal behaviors:** In order to accommodate a family member with OCD, the family may resist certain topics of conversation, restrict activities, and stay away from certain people, places, sounds, smells, or things.

Frustrated family members often try logical reasoning to no avail. Logic does nothing to break the OCD cycle.

TIP

Family members and partners of people with OCD should be educated about the OCD cycle in order to help their loved one. Family-based treatment is usually recommended for children and teens with OCD.

What outside challenges do you face that get in your way of getting treatment for your OCD? Write about them in Worksheet 5-2.

WORKSHEET 5-2 **My Reflections on External Obstacles to My Getting Treatment for OCD**

IN THIS CHAPTER

» Doing away with denial

» Blowing up change-blocking beliefs

» Looking for help in the wrong places

Chapter 6 Overcoming OCD's Obstacles Blocking Change

You're reading this book, so I'm going to make the wild assumption that you have some interest in learning about treating obsessive-compulsive disorder (OCD) and that you or someone you care about has symptoms. Those symptoms are causing distress, and you'd like to do something about that. In this chapter, I describe how to get ready for change and bust through any barriers that may be getting in your way.

Preparing for Change

Taking on OCD requires courage and stamina. Facing fears head on demands commitment. Many people with OCD struggle with facing change. In fact, the vast majority of people never seek treatment. But here you are and hopefully you're ready to make the choice. You can get better.

Most people move through several stages when they're starting to change either a bad habit, a way of thinking, or a behavior. To get you ready for action, the next sections detail the stages of change. Based on extensive studies by psychologists the stages are:

- **Precontemplation:** Denial of symptoms or the distress caused by them
- **Contemplation:** Thinking about changing and how to go about it
- **Action:** Doing the work necessary for change
- **Maintenance:** Keeping well by looking out for lapses

Precontemplation: Staying stuck with denial

Many people with OCD are in complete denial about their symptoms. They believe that their compulsive behaviors are perfectly normal, and they don't see any reason to change. I'm guessing you've moved out of denial. You realize that OCD is a problem for you and you're ready to tackle the next step, which is thinking about changing.

Contemplation: Thinking about the possibilities

In this stage of change, you begin to consider all your options. You realize that you have a problem and decide you need to work on it. The following questions may help you move forward:

- What would your life be like without the constant distress of OCD?
- Have you thought about the time you would save?
- Stress is a risk factor for many health conditions. Would your physical health benefit if you had less tension and worry?
- How would you go about finding help?
- Are there resources you already know about (see Chapter 7 for more about getting help)?
- Do you have people around you who want to see you get better?

After reading these questions, what thoughts do you have? Write about them in Worksheet 6-1.

Action: Moving forward with a plan

You've moved through thinking about change and challenging your change blocking thoughts and beliefs. You may be ready to start working by getting treatment for your OCD with the help of a mental health provider. Or perhaps you think your OCD is mild enough to try it out on your own.

Congratulations on your readiness to move forward! During the action stage of change, you develop specific goals for changing. Take it slowly and persistently. Change doesn't happen quickly. Expect some frustration and bumps along the way. Practice self-compassion. After all, you're taking a giant step!

Whether you plan to work with a therapist or try self-help, the chapters that follow can provide you or your therapist with specific techniques.

WORKSHEET 6-1 My Reflections on My Process of Changing My OCD

Maintenance: Keeping progress well oiled

Oil changes keep your car running smoothly. When you successfully treat your OCD and are basically in remission, a few strategies can help you keep yourself running smoothly, too.

During the maintenance stage of change, it's important to keep up a healthy lifestyle. In other words, eat right, exercise, get enough sleep, and engage in positive social interaction. Stress can lead to a brief return of symptoms and even total relapse. When inevitable times of stress occur, practice self-compassion. Overall, you can maintain your progress, but be on the lookout for situations that cause you discomfort. For more information about relapse prevention, see Chapter 20.

Overcoming Barriers to Change

Change is hard. OCD makes change especially challenging because you feel unsafe, distressed, and frightened if you don't respond to your obsessions with compulsive behaviors or thoughts. The following sections give you some tools to help you move through obstacles and progress to action.

Performing a cost-benefit analysis

Borrowed from the business world, the cost-benefit analysis is one of the best tools in psychology to help people make decisions. The exercise is used to help people look squarely at a problem and determine the relative costs and benefits of changing.

TIP

I highly recommend this technique for all sorts of problems that require a decision. From deciding which car to buy to whether to stay in a relationship, whether to give up eating candy, or whether to get treatment for OCD, the cost-benefit analysis is an easy, straightforward technique that helps clarify issues when making a decision.

The task is simple. On one side, list all the benefits of staying the same; on the other side, the costs. This exercise, to be effective, takes quite a bit of thinking. To help clarify, take a look at an example:

> Jeremy has OCD. He obsesses over the possibility of his family being harmed. His obsessions include people breaking into his house, his house burning down, or something else catastrophic due to his own negligence. He imagines family members injured or dead. Jeremy has an extensive security and monitoring system for his house. He owns a roof-top weather station in case of dangerous winds, rain, or snowstorms. He has immense quantities of emergency supplies. Since the birth of his children, Jeremy's symptoms have gotten worse. He spends hours every day checking and rechecking his systems and going through his supplies. His wife is ready to leave him if he doesn't get help.

Table 6-1 shows what Jeremy's cost-benefit analysis would be for deciding to get treatment.

TABLE 6-1 Jeremy's Sample Cost-Benefit Analysis for Deciding to Get Treatment

Benefits	Costs
I keep my family safe from break-ins, fire, and carbon dioxide poisoning.	My wife is about to leave me.
I know if bad weather is coming.	I don't have time to spend with my family.
If something happens, my family will be able to survive.	My work suffers because I'm always checking on the house.
I couldn't stand it if anything bad happened, so this keeps them all safe.	Lots of people think I'm weird.
Treatment would be too hard.	I'm worried all the time.
I need to do something to keep those thoughts from overwhelming me. Checking on safety gives me some relief.	I really can't remember the last time I relaxed and had fun.
	I can't keep my family safe if they leave me.

After completing his cost-benefit analysis, Jeremy is ready to start making a plan to get help for his OCD. He realizes that the cost of the time he spends "keeping his family safe" is that he doesn't really have time for a relationship with them.

Sometimes people find it difficult to come up with specific costs of OCD. They believe that changing is simply too dangerous or difficult. Here are some consequences of OCD that you may not have realized:

- Shame and embarrassment
- Feelings of not being normal
- Relationship troubles related to your OCD routines
- Problems making new friends
- Irritability
- Cracked hands from excessive cleaning or washing
- Financial costs from buying materials, underachievement at work, or missed days
- Avoidance of many activities because of OCD
- Avoidance of places
- Stress and anxiety
- Problems with travel because of contamination concerns
- Problems using restrooms
- Loss of precious time for enjoying life

Now, complete your own cost-benefit analysis in Worksheet 6-2. Spend some time thinking about all the possible costs and benefits when you're considering treatment for your OCD. If you have someone close to you whom you trust, consider asking them to participate in the exercise.

WORKSHEET 6-2 My Cost-Benefit Analysis for Deciding to Get Treatment

Benefits	Costs

TIP

After you complete your cost-benefit analysis, go back over the benefits. Are they really benefits? Reconsider each one and see if there is a cost involved.

Stopping self-defeating thinking

Fear of change increases self-defeating thinking. Those with OCD often have thoughts about their abilities that get in the way of treatment. Worksheet 6-3 lists some common self-defeating thoughts. Read through the list and check the ones that apply to you.

WORKSHEET 6-3 Self-Defeating Thoughts

Yes	No	Self-Defeating Thoughts
		My OCD is severe and I can't face the pain of changing.
		I will work on my OCD when I have time. Right now I'm too busy.
		If I can't be 100 percent better, I'd rather not try.
		OCD is a brain disease. There's no point in trying therapy.
		This treatment is too hard. I don't want to commit.
		I'm too depressed to try to work on my OCD.
		I might hurt someone I love or myself if I give up OCD.
		I doubt this treatment really works.
		Add your own self-defeating thought:
		Add your own self-defeating thought:

After you've identified your self-defeating thoughts, take some time to come up with some more reasonable replacement thoughts. Table 6-2 shows you some examples.

Decreasing change-stopping beliefs

A thought is simply a fleeting mental event. They come and go throughout each day. For example, if I make a spelling mistake while I'm writing, I might have a fleeting thought that says, "I can't believe I goofed up. I'm so careless."

That thought doesn't really mean that overall, in my life, I'm a careless person. I know that I'm reasonably conscientious even though I make careless mistakes sometimes. So, I don't have the belief that I'm a careless person.

REMEMBER

Beliefs are thoughts that you repeatedly have and assume are true. Beliefs influence the way you view the world. They act as filters through which you see reality.

TABLE 6-2 Replacing Self-Defeating Thoughts

Self-Defeating Thoughts	Healthier Alternatives
My OCD is severe and I can't face the pain of changing.	Although my OCD is severe, I can start my change very slowly.
I'll work on my OCD when I have time. Right now, I'm too busy.	My OCD takes up at least a couple of hours a day. Wouldn't that be nice to have that time back?
If I can't be 100 percent better, I'd rather not try.	That's my OCD thinking. There is no such thing as absolute perfection.
OCD is a brain disease. There's no point in trying therapy.	I've heard some medications help, and I've read that certain types of therapy help as well.
This treatment is too hard. I don't want to commit.	My life with OCD is pretty hard. I can tell my therapist about my fears, and they'll help me through this.
I'm too depressed to try to work on my OCD.	That may be true, but depression is a treatable mental health problem. It's an obstacle that I can overcome.
I might hurt someone I love or myself if I give up OCD.	This fear is part of my OCD. I know that these fears are unrealistic and unlikely to happen.
I doubt this treatment really works.	Multiple studies show that treatment for OCD is effective.

Certain beliefs interfere with choosing treatment for OCD and subsequent treatment success. The following change-stopping beliefs get in the way:

- **I'm inadequate.** OCD makes people feel like they can't handle everyday challenges. Being inadequate leads to lack of confidence. Therefore, people with OCD believe they can't face the difficulties involved in treatment.
- **I'm undeserving.** People with the undeserving belief are convinced that health and happiness are for others, not them. They feel uncomfortable when others offer to help and end up wallowing in their own misery.
- **I'm a victim.** This belief goes along with the OCD obsession about being overly responsible for bad events. Trauma is not a cause of OCD but a risk factor. Those who believe that they're victims usually have more severe symptoms along with a feeling of hopelessness about treatment. Victimhood also decreases a person's sense of control, which increases pessimism about the future.
- **I'm guilty.** Guilt and shame interfere with treatment. It pushes the belief that OCD is caused by a personal flaw. People who feel guilty also find themselves believing that somehow it's fair that they suffer.

If you suffer from change-stopping beliefs, try Worksheet 6-4. Read the challenges that pertain to your belief and then rewrite a more reasonable belief in the third column.

WORKSHEET 6-4 Challenging My Change-Stopping Beliefs

Self-Defeating Belief	Challenges	A More Reasonable Belief
I'm inadequate.	Am I really inadequate 100 percent of the time? Am I able to do anything at all? Have I accomplished things in the past? What evidence do I have that I'm adequate?	
I'm undeserving.	What really makes me undeserving? Doesn't everyone deserve a break? Do I have evidence that this is 100 percent true? Is this belief helpful?	
I'm a victim.	I know that bad things can happen, but sometimes good things happen, too. Can I recall at least one good thing that happened to me? This belief makes me stuck. With help, is it possible for me to make some start in recovery?	
I'm guilty.	This sounds like my OCD thinking. Is it a thought or a fact? Did I ask to have OCD? Is this all my fault? Am I guilty all the time? Do I have any evidence that maybe I'm okay?	

Do you have any change-blocking beliefs? Consider them in Worksheet 6-5 and reflect on how they may be getting in the way of starting treatment. Were you able to challenge them? How?

WORKSHEET 6-5 My Reflections on Change-Blocking Beliefs

Examining reassurance seeking

Asking for reassurance is a common OCD compulsion. It's designed to decrease anxiety by asking for love, validation, or comforting information. Most important, reassurance seeking is designed to remove the distress of uncertainty. Questions like the following make a person with OCD feel dependent on others:

- Are you sure the treatment will work?
- Can you guarantee that I'll be able to tolerate the distress?
- Will you help me get through this?

A major goal of treatment is to help those with OCD tolerate uncertainty. Reassurance seeking creates vulnerability and lack of confidence. See Chapter 2 for more information about compulsions and reassurance seeking.

Do you have someone in your life whom you ask for comfort, support, and validation? Do you think you're asking for too much reassurance? Reflect on these questions in Worksheet 6-6.

WORKSHEET 6-6 My Reflections on Reassurance Seeking

IN THIS CHAPTER

» Getting to know mental health professionals

» Questioning potential providers

» Opting for support from others

Chapter 7

Looking at Treatment Options

Obsessive-compulsive disorder (OCD) is a chronic and distressing mental health disorder. People with OCD spend considerable time each and every day having persistent obsessions followed by repetitive compulsive actions. There are evidence-based treatments available that can help people with OCD vastly improve the quality of their lives.

In this chapter, I explore a comprehensive cast of mental health characters and describe their training. I also detail the importance of specialized training in the procedures that have been shown to help those with OCD gain control over their symptoms.

Looking for a Professional

Although self-help and support groups can be a valuable part of recovery, in most cases people with OCD need professional help. The following sections describe the type of training to look for, the types of professionals available that may have the appropriate training, and how to navigate the healthcare system to find a good match for you.

TIP

Finding the right therapist is critical. OCD is a relentless cycle of distress that controls the lives of those afflicted. Specialized care is needed to help people with OCD improve the quality of their lives.

Types of professionals

Many people offer mental health treatment, but they aren't all the same. Before you start your search, check with your insurance company and see if they have a particular list of providers that you're required to go to in order to have the sessions covered. Most insurance companies have a variety of providers to choose from.

If you don't have coverage for mental health treatment, you may choose to pay out of pocket. The good news is that with exposure and response prevention (ERP) therapy, you can expect to have reduced symptoms in just a couple of months and good results in less than five months. People with high levels of social support and motivation can often experience symptom relief sooner. Of course, complex cases including multiple mental health conditions may take longer.

REMEMBER

OCD is best treated by evidence-based therapy including ERP and cognitive behavioral therapy (CBT). Medication may support treatment but is rarely enough without therapy.

The following professionals are licensed in their states to provide mental health services:

- **Counselors:** Most counselors have master's degrees in counseling, education, theology, or psychology. Their education and training vary widely. Some have excellent training in ERP and CBT. Ask about training and experience.
- **Psychiatrists:** Psychiatrists are trained medical doctors (MDs) who have additional training in the diagnosis and treatment of mental illness. Although they may be aware of ERP, most psychiatrists restrict their practices to biological treatments and don't offer psychotherapy. You may need to see a psychiatrist for medication management — be sure to ask if they have experience treating OCD. (See Chapter 15 for information about biological treatments for OCD.)
- **Psychologists:** Psychologists have a doctoral or master's degree and are very likely to have training in the evidence-based therapies for OCD. Most psychologists don't prescribe medication, but in some states, they do have that privilege.
- **Social workers:** Social workers have master's or doctoral degrees and have training in helping people access services, as well as conduct psychotherapy. Be sure to ask if they have the specialized training in ERP.

WARNING

Other people may advertise their proficiency in treating OCD, but be sure to find a licensed professional.

Professional training

There are several major approaches used by mental health professionals that provide different focuses of treatment. When you speak to a therapist, they can identify which approach they take to treat their clients. The following represent the most common schools of thought.

- **Psychodynamic therapy:** Emphasizes unconscious motives, childhood experiences, and the ways these factors influence current functioning.

- **Humanistic therapy:** Focuses on personal growth, unconditional positive regard, and allowing the client to set the path of therapy.
- **Existential therapy:** Looks at life's meaning, purpose, ultimate problems, freedom, and personal responsibility.
- **CBT:** Identifies thoughts and behaviors that lead to unhelpful feelings or actions. Variations of techniques based on the premise of CBT include ERP, dialectical behavior therapy (DBT), acceptance and commitment therapy (ACT), and habit reversal training (HRT).

TIP

The gold standard for treating OCD remains ERP within a broader CBT framework.

When you speak to a therapist, be sure to ask if they have training and experience in working with clients using ERP. If not, ask if they would be willing to get additional continuing education. Although other forms of therapy may help reduce some symptoms, ERP is the best treatment for OCD.

TECHNICAL STUFF

Training is offered by the International OCD Foundation (`https://iocdf.org`), through graduate programs, and at specialized centers across the United States. In addition, providers can access continuing education and seek supervision and consultation from their more experienced peers.

Asking the right questions

You've made the decision to seek professional help. Before making your first appointment, it's important to get some initial questions answered about costs, appointments, credentials, and experience. You can use Worksheet 7-1 to record the answers from any mental health provider you're considering.

WORKSHEET 7-1 Questions for a Mental Health Provider

Question	Answer
Are you accepting new patients?	
Do you take my insurance? If not, what is your fee?	
What are your hours of practice?	
How soon can I be seen?	

(continued)

WORKSHEET 7-1 ***(continued)***

Question	Answer
Do you practice telehealth?	
How long are your sessions?	
Do you have a cancellation fee?	
Do you have availability between sessions for emergencies?	
What is your approach to therapy?	
Do you administer ERP?	
Do you ever consider administering ERP outside of the office or through telehealth?	
Do you teach clients how to administer ERP for themselves?	
What is your experience treating OCD?	
Do you ever schedule multiple sessions in a week to administer ERP? If so, is that covered by insurance?	

TIP

Take the time to carefully choose a provider. Getting the right match is crucial for your recovery.

Beginning psychotherapy

During the first session, you can expect to be asked lots of questions. You may want to anticipate some of the questions by completing the following exercise.

WORKSHEET 7-2 **Preparing for Questions from Your Therapist**

Questions	Answers
What are your current symptoms?	
How severe are your symptoms?	
Do they interfere with your daily life?	
What triggers your symptoms?	
How do you handle your symptoms now?	
Do you have times when you are symptom free?	
How long have you been suffering from these symptoms?	
Have you had a history of other emotional issues?	
How is your physical health? Does your physical health impact your emotional health?	

(continued)

WORKSHEET 7-2 ***(continued)***

Questions	Answers
Have you ever had thoughts of harming yourself or others? Have you ever acted on these thoughts?	
Do you have a history of trauma?	
Do you work, go to school, or have other responsibilities? Have there been any recent changes in how you handle your responsibilities?	
Who lives in your home? Discuss your personal relationships. Are they healthy?	
Have you had mental health treatment in the past? Describe it.	
Do you have a family history of mental health problems?	
Is there anything else you might want to mention, such as using any substances to cope?	

REMEMBER

Please be open and honest with your therapist. They can't help you if you don't tell them your deepest concerns. Believe me, most therapists have heard many tragic, strange, weird, embarrassing, and scary stories. Yours is unlikely to be more shocking or worse than others.

When you choose a therapist, you need to consider if the relationship going forward is going to be beneficial. Having a good therapeutic relationship is critical to making progress in treatment.

Don't make any judgments after the first couple of sessions unless you absolutely feel that you and your therapist don't match. Around the third or fourth session, consider completing the following exercise in Worksheet 7-3.

WORKSHEET 7-3 Evaluating the Therapeutic Relationship

Question	Answer
Do I feel comfortable talking to my therapist?	
Do I feel safe telling my therapist things that are embarrassing?	
Do I feel criticized or judged?	
Does my therapist really listen and hear me?	
How do I feel after talking with my therapist?	
Does my therapist talk in jargon or in language that I can understand?	
Do I feel like we work together as a team?	
Do I think that we collaborated on setting goals?	
Do I feel safe during the sessions, even when things get scary?	
Do I feel like I am moving forward in my understanding and treating OCD?	

After completing Worksheet 7-3, what are your thoughts about your therapy? Worksheet 7-4 is a place for you to write about your thoughts. Consider showing your therapist your answers. Most therapists would welcome the feedback.

WORKSHEET 7-4 My Thoughts about Therapy

___

___

___

___

___

___

___

___

___

___

___

___

___

___

___

___

___

LESSONS LEARNED FROM PERFORMING ERP

One of the many benefits of being a psychologist is that I'm constantly learning from my clients. ERP involves building up trust and collaborating with a client on a plan of action. The treatment is based on very slowly guiding a client through exercises that cause distress. I started at a level the client was just a bit uncomfortable with and very gradually progressed to more difficult exposures. As a psychologist, I have to carefully assess the client's readiness, back down when needed, offer encouragement, and basically be a cheerleader throughout the process.

Most of the time, while doing ERP, I was an active participant. If the client had to touch garbage cans, I would be right there doing the same. I touched bird poop, held gooey substances, chanted bad words, ate meals on the floor, and spent lots of time flushing toilets, touching toilets, and even smelling some pretty gross stuff. Doing the ERP along with the client helped me, too.

I was kind of a squeamish young adult. I had an easy gag reflex and an aversion to dead or smelly things. Exposure throughout my life has helped increase my ability to tolerate all sorts of disgusting things. I've worked in clinics, schools, hospitals, and jails. Those involved exposure to all sorts of gross smells (vomit, urine, feces, sweat), bloody sights, vulgar language, and weird or violent behaviors. My life in semirural New Mexico has exposed me to snakes, bugs, rodents, skunks, and lots of roadkill. So as a mature adult, my tolerance has greatly increased. That's all because of my repeated exposure to the very things that earlier in my life made me very disturbed. The theory of gradual exposure works in real life.

Self-Help and Other Options

You are the number-one participant in treating your OCD. You can't send yourself into a repair shop and expect someone else to fix your problem. And there are no spectacular pills that eliminate OCD symptoms on the spot.

Whatever help you decide on seeking, you are going to be part of the team. There are no quick fixes and anyone who promises one is probably outright telling you a lie or, at the very least, exaggerating. Your job is to become your own advocate. And becoming educated about OCD is a very good start. You're reading this book, so you're well on your way to understanding and leading your own team.

As detailed in the section "Looking for a Professional," earlier in this chapter, getting an experienced, well-trained mental health professional is most often a great choice. However, other sources of help can boost professional help and, for some people with mild symptoms, be an alternative to psychotherapy.

WARNING

If you feel sad and hopeless about your OCD, have difficulty managing daily life, or have suicidal thoughts, I strongly urge you to get professional help. You may have depression, which makes taking on a challenge this difficult almost impossible. Talk to your healthcare provider.

Friends and family

Friends and/or family can offer emotional support and encourage treatment for OCD. They can encourage their loved one to complete ERP and celebrate when there is noticeable improvement. For those who want to offer help, it's important to understand the disorder and how they can inadvertently reinforce the OCD cycle.

REMEMBER

The OCD cycle begins with an obsessive thought, image, or urge that causes discomfort or distress. To decrease the distress, a compulsive action is completed. That compulsion gives a small amount of relief, which reinforces the action or behavior. Thus, the cycle continues.

WARNING

It's quite common to find family members inadvertently reinforcing OCD. They accommodate their loved one's wishes by excessively cleaning, checking, reassuring, or participating in ritualistic behavior. This is done in an attempt to make their loved one feel better.

Friends and family members need education about how they can set sensitive and empathetic boundaries. Families are frequently a part of OCD treatment because of their innocent participation in compulsions, which actually makes OCD worse.

Sometimes a friend or family member can act as a coach during ERP sessions. That coach can be a huge benefit when you practice ERP on your own. Before you consider choosing someone you know to help you out, consider the following characteristics of a good coach:

- Most important, they're willing to become educated about OCD and ERP.
- They are compassionate and realize that OCD is a difficult disorder to treat.
- They're very calm and patient. ERP takes time. There are inevitable frustrations.
- They're able to laugh along with you when humorous moments come up, because they frequently do during ERP.
- They have the time available in their schedule. ERP may take several hours a week to perform and sometimes more in the early stages.
- Oh, and they should be willing and able to tolerate some pretty gross stuff!

If you have a person in mind, be sure to ask them if they really have the time and commitment to support you. If not, your therapist may have some suggestions on how you can perform ERP without a coach.

Online support and support groups

Online support and treatment surged as an alternative during the COVID-19 pandemic and has since revolutionized psychological treatment around the world. OCD treatment offered online is now considered an evidence-based treatment that improves access worldwide to those who live outside areas that have specialists. Usually less expensive than individual therapy, professionally run treatment groups are also available.

TIP

I recommend the International OCD Foundation as a reliable referral source. Head to `https://iocdf.org/ocd-finding-help/supportgroups` to find support groups.

In addition to online treatment by providers, support groups offer people with OCD connections with others. Support groups are moderated either by specialists or, more frequently, by others who suffer from OCD. They reduce isolation and stigma and can provide hope. Participants share stories, coping mechanisms, and ERP experiences.

Support groups shouldn't serve as a substitute for therapy, but they can help boost motivation, encourage commitment, and help prevent relapse.

WARNING

Be careful about sharing personal information online. That's especially true when accessing online support groups that aren't affiliated with a professional organization. Some so-called support groups offer unhelpful advice, give misinformation, or sell products or services that aren't likely to help. They may also increase anxiety, hopelessness, and breach privacy.

After considering all the options for help, do you have an action plan? If so, describe it in Worksheet 7-5. If not, write down why. Maybe you need more information. Parts 3, 4, and 5 detail specific treatments for OCD.

WORKSHEET 7-5 My Action Plan for Getting Treatment for OCD

3 First Choice: Exposure and Response Prevention

IN THIS PART . . .

Understand how exposure and response prevention (ERP) works.

Recognize the pluses and minuses of ERP.

Decide if ERP is right for you.

Start an ERP experiment.

Dig deep into your obsessions and compulsions and develop an ERP plan.

IN THIS CHAPTER

» Getting the gist of ERP

» Finding out how ERP works

» Deciding if ERP is for you

Chapter 8

Exploring Exposure and Reviewing Response

Exposure and response prevention (ERP) was first developed during the middle of the last century. Prior to that, obsessive-compulsive disorder (OCD) was basically considered untreatable. Years of therapy did very little to reduce the suffering of those with OCD. Over the decades, there have been modifications and additions to the original treatment. However, the basic premise of ERP has remained the same.

In this chapter, I provide examples and explanations on how ERP works. With that understanding, you can make an informed decision about whether to pursue this form of therapy. If you choose to go forward, Chapters 9 and 10 guide you slowly and safely through the process. If you decide that you're not ready to undertake ERP, Parts 4 and 5 provide alternatives to ERP.

REMEMBER

To get the most out of ERP, I recommend consulting an experienced mental health professional. They can help you get started. If your OCD is mild, you may only need a few sessions. A few people with very mild OCD understand the concept and can apply it themselves, but you should seek professional help if you don't get better.

Exposure and Response Prevention Basics

Exposure and response prevention involves triggering an obsession and then delaying, changing, or eventually eliminating the compulsion that provides some relief. In this section, I detail the process through an example.

When you were a kid, did you ever hear the expression, "If you step on a crack, you'll break your mother's back?" Another similar saying is, "If you step on a line you'll break your father's spine."

Apparently, those sayings came from ancient times when people believed that there might be evil spirits within cracks in the earth. They believed that stepping on cracks could release those spirits and cause harm. You may be wondering what in the world stepping on cracks has to do with ERP.

Those harmless childhood superstitions are good examples of how ERP works. The obsessions, in this case, are thoughts about possibly harming a loved one. The compulsions could be simply avoiding stepping on lines or cracks or having some ritual that needs to be done to "undo" the act or asking others for reassurance that they remain okay. For more information about obsessions and compulsions, refer to Chapter 2.

Exposing exposure

Don't worry, you don't have to take off your clothes during exposure. Basically, exposure means that you come in contact with the thoughts, cues, events, situations, or other triggers that lead you to an obsessional fear. For example, if you're terrified of touching doorknobs for fear of getting sick, the very sight of a doorknob may increase your distress. In addition, you may anticipate having to touch a doorknob when you're thinking about going out of the house, or recall touching a doorknob in the past and feeling uneasy. Exposure to a doorknob would include looking at or touching one.

Take the example of stepping on a crack causing harm to your family. If this were a true obsession, the very thought of cracks might makes you uneasy. Exposures generally start with something pretty easy and gradually get more difficult. Here are some theoretical steps for this particular obsession:

- Spend ten minutes looking at pictures of cracks on sidewalks, roads, or paths.
- Walk on an extremely cracked surface.
- Touch a crack with your toe.
- Step on a crack with your whole foot.
- Stop and step on a crack with both feet.
- Say out loud, I stepped on a crack and now my family might get hurt.
- Stand on a crack for five minutes.
- Stand on a crack for five minutes without wearing shoes.
- Travel out of the neighborhood and step on cracks.
- Sit down for one minute on top of a crack.

TIP

You may be thinking that some of these exposures seem, well, a bit excessive. That's how exposure works. By the time someone is sitting down on a cracked sidewalk, there's usually some laughing and giggling going on. That's the opposite of fear and worry.

Pausing or preventing response

Response prevention involves not performing the usual compulsion that follows an obsession. So, if your normal compulsion is an extensive cleaning routine in response to the obsessive feeling of contamination, you would avoid cleaning. In this case, you might avoid cleaning for 30 minutes or an hour. Or your cleaning time would be reduced. If you normally clean for an hour, you would only clean for 30 minutes.

In the case of stepping on a crack, avoidance is the most common compulsion. So, during response prevention, instead of avoiding cracks, you would practice stepping directly on cracks. This takes time and practice.

Other compulsions would also be prevented. For example, if you step on a crack and then have to text family members to see if they are okay, that would have to be delayed or stopped. If you have a certain prayer or mental ritual that follows the crack stepping, that too would be delayed and then stopped. Gradually, you'd get to the point where you could step on a crack without having the obsession.

How ERP Works

Practice, practice, practice. Everyone learns best when they spend time repeating something they need to learn over and over again. Some research suggests that to become pretty good at a skill you need to practice every day for about a month, around 20 hours or so. To become exceptional, many suggest 10,000 hours. That doesn't always fit and there are many exceptions, but you get the idea.

Think about your own OCD. How many hours have you "practiced" your OCD? I bet well over a hundred. Maybe looking back, you've spent a thousand hours involved in obsessions and compulsions. If you've had OCD for more than a couple of years, the hours would easily exceed 1,000.

Face it, your OCD is pretty firmly ingrained. The task of practicing ERP is to unlearn what OCD taught you and to learn new ways of thinking and behaving.

Think about how OCD has interfered with your life. Come up with a rough estimate of all the hours you've spent among your obsessions and compulsions and write about that in Worksheet 8-1. Does looking at that information in writing make you want to make changes?

TIP

Be patient with yourself. It takes effort and hours of practice to unlearn the cycle of OCD. The good news is that when you really understand and experiment with ERP, your symptoms will decrease.

WORKSHEET 8-1 **My Reflections on the Time I've Spent with My Obsessions and Compulsions**

____

____

____

____

____

____

____

____

____

____

____

____

____

____

____

____

____

Learning and reinforcement

A basic premise in psychology and learning is reinforcement. There are two kinds of reinforcement, positive and negative. Both types of reinforcement strengthen the response. If you reward an action with something positive, that action is more likely to occur again and more frequently. Here are a few examples of positive reinforcement:

- A paycheck for working at a job
- A bonus for working beyond expectations
- A sticker for turning in homework
- A treat for your dog when they sit or stay
- A discount on your car insurance for being a good driver
- Praise for being kind

Positive reinforcement doesn't fuel OCD. However, after treatment is started, you can use positive reinforcement to continue your progression through treatment. For example, you might reward yourself with a great meal after completing ERP.

OCD is driven by another type of reinforcement called *negative reinforcement.* Simply put, negative reinforcement occurs when you have an uncomfortable feeling, and then do something, and the bad feeling goes away. That something you do when you feel distress is also more likely to occur again and more frequently. Here are a few situations in which negative reinforcement occurs:

- Someone feels hunger pain and then eats and feels better.
- A baby cries, making people feel on edge, so they feed the baby and the crying stops.
- You have an urge to shout obscenities during a church service, you feel guilty, you pray, and your guilt is temporarily quelled.
- You have a splinter that hurts, you dig it out with tweezers, and you feel immediate relief.
- You feel stressed, drink a glass of wine, and you feel less stressed.
- You feel contaminated and then wash your hands and then you don't feel contaminated.

OCD involves obsessions followed by distress. That distress is uncomfortable. The distress is relieved by performing an action or compulsion. Therefore, those compulsions are more likely to reoccur. OCD compulsions are negatively reinforced.

Gradually deconditioning

Deconditioning is the process in which connections between an obsession and the associated compulsion is disrupted or weakened. During ERP, the deconditioning occurs when the obsession is triggered and the compulsion is not performed. The person feels distress but does not engage in the regular response. Over time, the distress reduces. Gradually, with lots of practice, relearning occurs. To clarify, here are some examples of how deconditioning works.

- Gayle obsesses about symmetry and keeps the cans in her cupboard in a certain order. During an early session of ERP, she is asked to purposely move a few cans out of order. She feels distress. After five minutes of having the cans out of order, her distress gradually diminishes. This process is repeated and each trial is made slightly more difficult. Gradually, she learns that having cans out of order is no big deal.
- Samuel worries excessively about being clean. He has detailed rituals that he must follow before, during, and after each shower. He showers twice a day, and each shower takes more than an hour. Throughout the day, he also engages in excessive handwashing. During ERP, he is instructed to slowly decrease the time he spends showering and washing. At first, he's sure that he'll get sick and his anxiety is extremely high. Over time, he begins to understand that reducing his compulsive behavior doesn't cause illness.
- Jack fears harming his children. He believes that he will lose control and possibly throw something at them. He compulsively prays for multiple hours each day and tries to avoid his kids as much as possible. During ERP, he is asked to imagine a scene in which he hurts one of his kids. Following that exposure, he must refrain from praying. After multiple experiments, he learns that his kids are okay without his compulsive praying.

TECHNICAL STUFF

If someone breaks a leg and has a cast on for a couple of months, the strength in the leg decreases because the person is restricted and can't use their muscles. That gradual decline in physical functioning that occurs as a result of inactivity is called *deconditioning*. Similarly, in ERP, the relationship between an obsession and the resulting compulsion weakens or declines. That's because during ERP, compulsive behavior is blocked or inactivated and eventually weakened.

Slowly reconditioning

When ERP works, the brain begins the process of rewiring or reconditioning. The process usually starts with an easy-to-handle level of distress. When you're able to handle or tolerate that level of distress, ERP gradually moves on to more distressing practice. Repeated practice, which includes homework, is essential for ERP to work. Eventually, the obsessions, with their feared consequences, are deconditioned and new learning occurs.

TIP

One important key to successful ERP is to continue to practice until it gets boring or even silly. When you can perform the act without feeling distress, you know that ERP has worked.

Have you ever experienced deconditioning? Maybe it was fear of the water or flying. Describe it in Worksheet 8-2.

WORKSHEET 8-2 My Reflections on Deconditioning

DECONDITIONING STAGE FRIGHT

I was an extremely shy child. In school, I rarely raised my hand and when I answered, my answers were as short as possible. In college, I avoided taking classes that required oral presentations. When I had to give a talk, the buildup would include digestive problems, fear, sweating, and trembling. I dreaded every minute. However, as time went on and I did more presentations, I gradually realized that once I got started, the presentations usually went pretty well.

But my reluctance to speak in public persisted. Sometime in my late 20s, I was convinced to make a presentation at a large professional conference. The weeks and days before, my nerves were horrible. As I was presenting, the audience warmly responded. They laughed at my jokes and applauded when I finished. That experience didn't "cure" my shyness, but it pushed me forward to make more presentations. Now, I'm able to enjoy giving workshops to hundreds of people without fear. What happened? My fear was deconditioned and slowly reconditioned with joy.

Types of exposure

There are different ways to perform exposures. The most common form is real-life exposure. It involves confronting the feared situation. A common real-life exposure for those with contamination fears is touching the feared object, such as a bathroom stall, doorknob, or handrail in a public place.

For those with fears of harming someone else, shouting out obscenities in church, or running over someone with a car, real-life exposure obviously isn't feasible. Instead, *imaginal exposure* is used. In this case, ERP may involve thinking about the feared situation or writing out a script. The exposure is repeated until the experience of distress is decreased.

Virtual reality (VR) can replicate real-life scenarios in a safe way. With the addition of artificial intelligence (AI), ERP can be managed and monitored. Physiological changes such as heart rate, body temperature, or eye tracking can be evaluated, and exposures can gradually get more difficult without becoming overwhelming.

Think about your own OCD obsessions and compulsions. Which type of exposure makes most sense for you? Why? Write your thoughts in Worksheet 8-3.

WORKSHEET 8-3 My Reflections on Exposures That May Work for Me

The Risks and Benefits of ERP

Hundreds of studies over the last 50 years consistently support ERP as a highly effective method for treating OCD. If that's the case, why do so many people still struggle with OCD? Shouldn't everyone with OCD seek out this powerful tool?

Counting up the costs

Of those people who are able to find a therapist trained in administering ERP, many drop out prematurely. That's because, in order for ERP to work, the client must experience significant distress. Even with the promise that the temporary state of distress eventually lessens, some people don't believe they can tolerate those feelings even for a short period of time.

TIP

As a psychologist with years of experience, I have managed in most cases to support people through OCD treatment by starting with extremely easy ERP exercises. Chapter 9 offers more information on how to slowly and gently begin ERP.

Another cost of ERP is time. ERP may need to be conducted more than once a week and sometimes takes longer than the standard therapy session. In addition, homework outside of therapy is required so that the skills learned in session are applied in real life.

Adding up the benefits

The biggest benefit of ERP is that it works. Studies show that it works better than medication alone and better than other treatments. Most people who complete treatment experience a significant reduction in symptoms. ERP doesn't require a deep dive into the past. It's an active present focused treatment with immediate benefits.

ERP addresses the root causes of OCD. Therefore, successful treatment tends to last. Many clients after completing treatment are able to do ERP on their own, making professional intervention unnecessary.

ERP provides the client with a sense of confidence in their ability to handle distress and uncertainty. This empowerment increases the quality of their lives and frees up time for relationships, work, and recreation.

Deciding if ERP is for you

Any major decision requires careful analysis. Choosing ERP as a treatment for your OCD should be based on your own situation, tolerance for distress, and desire to face your fears. Worksheet 8-4 helps you clarify your reasons for and against ERP. Under Benefits, list all the reasons you can think of for starting ERP therapy. Under Costs, consider all the reasons for your hesitation.

WORKSHEET 8-4 My Cost/Benefit Analysis of ERP

Benefits	Costs

After completing the cost-benefit analysis in Worksheet 8-4, what is your decision? Why? Write about your decision in Worksheet 8-5.

WORKSHEET 8-5 My Reflections on Whether ERP Is Right for Me

TIP

If you decide that ERP just isn't for you right now, no worries — there are other treatments for OCD. The next section briefly describes them and refers you to other chapters in the book for more information.

A Brief Look at Other Treatment Options

Although ERP is considered the gold standard for treating OCD, there are other options that can be used alone or in combination with ERP. The most common alternative is cognitive therapy (CT). In fact, cognitive therapy is often used in conjunction with ERP. Cognitive therapy examines how thinking affects feelings. People with OCD have some common distortions in their thinking and faulty beliefs. Chapters 11 and 12 show you how to challenge distorted thinking patterns.

Dialectical behavior therapy (DBT) was originally developed for people with severe emotional distress. However, this skills-based program can give people with OCD help with managing the intense anxiety they experience because of their obsessive thinking. Distress tolerance, methods of self-soothing, and acceptance of reality are DBT skills I explain in Chapter 13.

Instead of controlling distressing obsessions, acceptance and commitment therapy (ACT) helps people with OCD allow thoughts to come and go and accept them as transient mental events. The primary goal of ACT is to encourage people to live value-driven lives despite having distressing thoughts and emotions. Chapter 14 offers some ACT exercises and examples.

TECHNICAL STUFF

Mental health professionals love initials. ERP, CT, DBT, and ACT all fall under the broad umbrella of cognitive behavioral therapy (CBT). All these treatments involve changing the way people think and behave in order to improve emotional and mental health. Don't worry too much about memorizing which set of initials means what.

Biological treatments for OCD are described in Chapter 15. Medication for a small group of people with OCD may be all that they need to feel significantly better. However, it isn't considered a first-line treatment. In my experience, certain medications can help people get through ERP treatment. In addition, the science of brain stimulation is constantly improving. I describe the latest treatments, as well as why they may be used.

After considering all options, which treatment path do you plan to take? Explain why in Worksheet 8-6.

WORKSHEET 8-6 My Reflections on the Treatment I Plan to Pursue

IN THIS CHAPTER

» Getting to know your obsessions and compulsions

» Taking baby steps

» Figuring out how ERP works for you

Chapter 9

Warming Up to Exposure and Response Prevention

Imagine a friend of yours who has a deep-seated fear of water. The thought of going in or near a body of water is absolutely terrifying. Your friend just found out that they won an all-inclusive cruise to the Caribbean. The trip is in six months. Your friend begs you to help them overcome their fear.

Using your own common sense, what would you do? Would you take them out into the middle of the ocean and drop them in? Of course not. You might start by taking them to a shallow pool and having them dangle their feet. Eventually you might encourage them to actually get into the shallow end of a pool and stand. A walk around a beach might be next.

You get the idea: slow and gradual. Exposure and response prevention (ERP) should follow that same sort of path. One of the main reasons that most people drop out of treatment for obsessive-compulsive disorder (OCD) is fear. In this chapter, I offer you the chance to dangle your feet into ERP treatment.

Identifying Your Obsessions and Compulsions

REMEMBER

Obsessions are repeated, unwelcome thoughts, images, or impulses that cause distress. Commonly, they're related to contamination, worry about danger, symmetry, harm to others, perfectionism, or moral depravity. These thoughts come into your consciousness without consent, disrupting your day. They're powerful and very difficult to ignore. They aren't everyday worries. Instead, they feel extremely distressful, unreasonable, or even irrational.

REMEMBER

Compulsions are the actions or behaviors that you do to relieve the anxiety or distress that follows the obsession. Compulsions can be overt acts such as washing hands, moving in a particular way, or arranging items in a certain order. Or they can be covert acts such as avoiding something, praying, or repeating things in your mind.

TIP

Chapter 2 offers an exhaustive list of obsessions and compulsions. If you completed the exercises in that chapter, you may want to review them. If you didn't, a quick read of the chapter may help you recognize your own obsessions and compulsions.

Worksheet 9-1 helps you identify your obsessions and compulsions. When you experience an obsessive thought, image, or impulse, jot it down. Then write down the compulsive action you took or wanted to take to bring down your distress. Finally, rate your distress on what I call the ugh factor. The scale ranges from 0 to 10, where 0 is no distress, 5 is moderate distress, and 10 is very upsetting. For now, don't worry about the rating, just estimate the level of distress. (See "Considering the ugh factor," later in this chapter, for more information.)

To get you started, Table 9-1 gives you an example.

TABLE 9-1 Keeping Track of Obsessions and Compulsions

Obsessions	Compulsions	Ugh Factor (0–10)
I'm sure I left the doors unlocked.	I repeatedly check the locks and monitor my security cameras.	8
If I touch something in a public bathroom, I'll get sick.	I avoid bathrooms to the point of physical discomfort. If bathrooms are unavoidable, I repeatedly wash and sanitize my hands.	10
If I'm near someone disabled, I might get contaminated and become disabled myself.	I scan the environment for people in wheelchairs and avoid close contact with people with disabilities.	5
I must always be perfect at work.	I redo my work to make sure it's done right.	4
When I look at people around me, I often see them naked. I must be some kind of pervert.	I avoid people as much as possible. I pray to God for forgiveness multiple times a day.	8
I constantly worry that I might lose control in public and soil myself.	Wherever I go, I always find the nearest bathroom. I sometimes wear pads to protect me, even though I've never had an accident.	6

TIP

If you're already in therapy, discuss this exercise with your therapist. If you aren't in therapy, it may be a good time to consider that option. (See Chapter 7 for ways to find a good therapist.) ERP is almost always best done in conjunction with a mental health professional.

Now, it's your turn. Give yourself some time to think about Worksheet 9-1. Don't rush — it's important that you're honest. Record your thoughts over the course of at least a week.

WORKSHEET 9-1 **Keeping Track of Obsessions and Compulsions**

Obsessions	Compulsions	Ugh Factor (0–10)

What are your thoughts after logging your obsessions and compulsions for a week? Write about them in Worksheet 9-2.

WORKSHEET 9-2 **My Reflections on Logging My Obsessions and Compulsions**

Choosing Your Challenge

The best way to begin ERP is to start with a very easy challenge. There are several reasons for this strategy:

- By starting with a fairly simple, slightly distressing obsession, you can experience success without severe discomfort.
- Doing fairly easy ERP helps you understand the concept behind the process.
- After mastering a few simple exposures, you'll have more confidence in later exercises in which you may experience more distress.
- This gradual approach begins to rewire your brain, which improves your chances to progress through the treatment successfully.

When considering what challenge to start with, begin with rating the amount of distress you feel. The next section describes, in more detail, the ugh factor and how it should guide you in your decision making.

Considering the ugh factor

Think of the ugh factor as your personal OCD thermometer. This thermometer is a measurement of your level of anxiety or distress. The higher the number or temperature, the more distress. The ugh factor increases your awareness of distress and helps you understand it as a temporary state that eventually decreases over time. The ugh factor also gives you a tool to quantify your distress at the beginning of an exposure, during an exposure, and after an exposure.

The ugh factor is a measure of distress on a scale from 0 to 10. Here's an idea of what each rating represents, but feel free to adjust it to your own levels of discomfort:

Rating	What It Means
0	No distress at all.
1	Very slight, almost nonexistent unease.
2	A small feeling of unease.
3	Mild distress.
4	Noticeable distress, enough to be completely aware of bad feelings.
5	Moderate distress.
6	Significant distress; disturbing physical symptoms such as a rapid heartbeat, muscle tightness, or stomach upset.
7	Starting to interfere with normal functioning, high distress.
8	Feeling overwhelmed and close to panic.
9	Unable to function in a normal way; extreme distress.
10	Loss of control; an extreme level of panic.

Unlike a thermometer for temperature, the ugh factor relies on your own interpretation of your feelings. Don't worry too much about being totally accurate — just use this as a tool to help you get through an exposure exercise and eventually monitor your progress.

TECHNICAL STUFF

In traditional ERP treatment, the ugh factor is called the *subjective units of distress scale* (SUDS). It's often a scale from 0 to 100. Recent research has found that the measure doesn't do a good job of measuring distress related to ERP. I find the name a bit too jargony for my taste and believe that a more straightforward name and a short range (0–10) works just fine.

Identifying your triggers

The triggers of OCD obsessions vary greatly across different types of obsessions. Think for a moment about what situation, feeling, or sight usually comes before your obsessions. To get you started, here are some examples:

- Conflicts with others
- Feelings of uncertainty
- Unexpected trauma
- Crowds
- Financial worries
- Images of harming someone
- Being sick or in pain
- Impulses to do something morally reprehensible
- Worries about not getting something done correctly
- Becoming aware of a certain sound, smell, or bodily sensation
- Doctors' offices or hospitals
- Things being out of order
- Certain places
- Being in an unfamiliar place or situation
- Making mistakes
- Feeling inadequate
- Lack of sleep
- Chronic stress
- Hunger
- Transitions in life (job, family, home)
- Changes in routines

Think about times when your obsessions have been dominant. Jot them down in Worksheet 9-3 and identify any possible triggers.

WORKSHEET 9-3 **My Reflections on My Triggers**

Starting slowly

Choose one obsessive thought that has a fairly low ugh factor, below 5. Here are a few examples to get you started:

- » Ruben is terrified that he might leave his house unlocked. He spends hours every day checking locks on the doors and windows. He rates his distress about the safety of his house as an ugh factor of 10. He also worries about keeping the outdoor shed locked, but not quite as much as his home. Still, he checks the lock on the shed a couple of times each day. His distress over the shed is more like an ugh factor of 4. For this exercise, he chooses to work on his fear of keeping the shed locked.
- » Marta believes that she can become contaminated by touching doorknobs, shaking hands, using public restrooms, sitting in waiting rooms, and accidentally bumping into people. Her distress about being contaminated is at least an ugh factor of 8. She also washes her hands after touching any of the appliances in her kitchen. But she isn't as stressed by touching things in her house. She rates her ugh factor of those obsessive thoughts as 3. Therefore, she will begin ERP by touching kitchen appliances.

» Ezra has obsessive thoughts about his partner, Mateo, cheating on him or leaving him. When Ezra's partner is at work he worries. He texts Mateo dozens of times a day to make sure that he's okay. When Mateo goes to the gym, Ezra is sure he's having an affair. Mateo is getting pretty annoyed by the constant interruptions. When Mateo travels, Ezra's distress is extreme. He rates business trips as the worst possible anxiety, an ugh factor at least 10. Ezra considers how much distress he feels when Mateo is away and decides to work on the obsessions that happen while he's at work.

Think about your own obsessions and choose one that increases your distress, but not too much. Write about it in Worksheet 9-4.

WORKSHEET 9-4 **Choosing an Obsession to Work On**

Changing Compulsions

For most people with OCD, an obsession causes distress, which then leads to some act — either overt or covert — that decreases the distress temporarily. Changing the way you respond to an obsession is a critical part of ERP. The purpose of this exercise is for you to begin to understand the process of ERP and, most important, to be successful.

Trying for seconds or minutes

For your first practice with ERP, pick an obsession, trigger it, and delay your usual compulsion. The practice of delaying your compulsion should start out very slowly. Try using a timer and set it for 30 seconds. How did that feel? Do you think you can bump that up to a minute?

Before you begin, Table 9-2 is an example of Marta touching her kitchen appliances (see "Starting slowly," earlier in this chapter). Marta has obsessions about becoming contaminated. She chooses to try to delay her normal handwashing routine by one minute.

TABLE 9-2 Delaying My Compulsion

Time	Obsession	Ugh Factor (0–10)
Start	If I touch my appliances, I'll get sick unless I wash my hands.	3
30 seconds	I really want to wash my hands.	6
1 minute	I feel really gross, but I made it.	3

Now, Marta should repeat the same exposure until her ugh factor after 30 seconds comes down to about 3. Multiple repetitions of this exposure will eventually become easy for her. Then she should gradually increase the delay time.

Now give it a try and record your obsession and ugh factor in Worksheet 9-5. In case you want to increase the amount of time you delay your compulsion, some extra rows are included.

WORKSHEET 9-5 Delaying My Compulsion

Time	Obsession	Ugh Factor (0–10)
Start		
30 seconds		
1 minute		
2 minutes		
3 minutes		
5 minutes		

REMEMBER

Pick an obsession that doesn't make you too upset. I want you to experience success so that you can understand the process of ERP.

TIP

The ultimate goal is to have an obsessive thought without performing a compulsion at all. However, in the beginning of treatment, a few minutes or so is just fine. Take the win.

Changing some other aspect of the compulsion

Another way to battle your OCD is to simply change the way you respond to your obsession. For example, if you wash your hands for five minutes with a particular kind of soap, change the soap, or decrease the time washing to four minutes, then three minutes.

Here are some other changes you may want to try:

- » Changing the speed of the compulsion (slowing it down or speeding it up).
- » Changing the numbers of your compulsion. For example, if you must count or repeat things a certain number of times, add or subtract a few numbers.
- » Changing the location of your compulsion. Wash in the bathroom instead of the kitchen.
- » Changing the order of your compulsions. For example, if you must go in and out of a door in a particular way, do it the opposite way.
- » Changing the covert thoughts, prayers, or chants.
- » Changing the objects you use in your compulsion. For example, if you need to tap on a particular surface, tap somewhere else.
- » Changing the direction of the compulsion, part your hair on the other side or change the order of something you feel compelled to do.
- » Doing the compulsion in the wrong way, out of order, or incompletely.

Practice changing your compulsions. This will help you to break through those rigid patterns and decrease the power of your obsessions. In Worksheet 9-6, jot down your obsession followed by your compulsion and the change you made to your regular compulsion.

WORKSHEET 9-6 Changing My Compulsion

Obsession	Regular Compulsion	Change

Repeating the Challenge

If you were learning to ski during your first lesson, the instructor wouldn't take you all the way up the mountain to ski the double black diamond runs. You'd probably first practice the technique on the slight incline of the bunny hill. Maybe in your second or third lesson, you'd venture up the chair lift — but not too far, and not too steep. You'd likely take many lessons to reach the most difficult trails.

That's the way ERP works. Start slowly and gradually, then make your exposures more difficult. By now, you should have spent some time experimenting and exploring the procedure. You should understand the principle of ERP so you can take it to the next level. If you haven't done the previous exercises, do those before proceeding with this section.

Tracking the ugh factor

The ugh factor is your instructor to guide you through the ERP process. It's a way to identify distress and keep the exposures at a manageable level. When people become overwhelmed during exposure, that's when they frequently drop out of treatment. The ugh factor gives you and your therapist information so that you can monitor your distress.

In addition, when ERP is working, the ugh factor starts to decrease. So, it's a great way to track progress. (Turn to Chapter 10 for more information about using the feedback provided by the ugh factor.)

Stepping it up

The next step in ERP is to pick another challenge. Again, make sure that the challenge is a relatively easy one for you. Don't try to master your OCD during the second experiment. Take your time — there is no instant cure. Be patient.

Ezra obsesses about the possibility that his partner, Mateo, is going to leave or cheat on him (see "Starting slowly," earlier in this chapter). Prior to starting ERP, Ezra would text Mateo dozens of times a day. Mateo felt smothered and irritated by the constant interruptions.

Like many people with OCD, pressure from a family member pushes Ezra to start treatment. He and his therapist agree that Ezra should text Mateo only eight times a day. During the first few trials, Ezra's ugh factor reached a high of 10. He didn't realize how much limiting those texts would bother him. Gradually, over a week, his ugh factor decreased to 4.

After talking it over with his therapist, Ezra decides to decrease his texts to one in the morning, one at lunchtime, and one in the late afternoon. He agreed that texting three times a day would be an appropriate number of times. However, his ugh factor went to 10 again and stayed that high during multiple trials.

Ezra, his therapist, and Mateo agreed to upping the number of texts to five a day. That seemed to work fine and Ezra's ugh factor decreased to 2. To make sure that ERP was successful, the number of texts slowly decreased by one. That gave Ezra time to handle the stress of fewer communications throughout the day.

REMEMBER

Take the time for ERP to work. If you feel too much distress, decrease the difficulty of the task. The purpose is to be successful and decrease suffering. It takes time and patience.

Reviewing the Process

ERP retrains and rewires the brain. Through repeated trials, anxiety and distress decrease. Think of it learning to ride a bike. You begin extremely fearful and wobbly and probably fall off a few of times. You need lots of practice to gain skills. It doesn't happen immediately. But gradually, your fear decreases and your confidence increases.

The process of ERP is simple and makes common sense. But don't underestimate the power of fear. ERP takes courage and persistence. Work slowly and celebrate every success. Stay with the process, and you'll get better.

How did you feel trying out ERP for the first time? Do you feel confident that you're ready to commit to ERP? Why or why not? Reflect on that in Worksheet 9-7 and discuss any concerns that you're having with your therapist.

WORKSHEET 9-7 My Reflections on Trying ERP

IN THIS CHAPTER

» Stacking up obsessions

» Keeping track of progress

» Solving ERP problems

Chapter 10

Moving On with Exposure and Response Prevention

Your brain is wired to be on the lookout for danger. That built in alarm system keeps you safe from saber-toothed tigers and poisonous snakes. When you have obsessive-compulsive disorder (OCD), your alarm system is super sensitive. Sirens go off when you're faced with the very thought of something dangerous in your environment.

Exposure and response prevention (ERP) helps you reset your overactive alarm. In order to do that, you have to have direct experiences with what you fear through *experiential learning.* Just as the name implies, experiential learning is learning by doing. Following the experience, you reflect on what happened and how it felt.

In this chapter, I guide you through the hard work of ERP. Expect to feel some anxiety and distress — but those difficult feelings are fleeting, and they decrease as you learn through experience. You will survive and stay safe throughout ERP. You just have to be willing to do these exercises repeatedly in order for exposure to work. Trust me: The journey is worth it.

Writing an Exposure Hierarchy

The experiences in ERP gradually increase in intensity. *Gradually* is the key word here. You don't want to jump out of an airplane if you're afraid of heights. You may want to first stand on the second step of a ladder. In this section, you create your own exposure ladder, with gentle steps leading to a greater challenge.

Thinking about your OCD theme

OCD comes in an infinite number of flavors. However, in most cases, there is an underlying theme or subject matter (see Chapter 2). Here are the most common categories:

- Fear of contamination
- Worry about doing something inappropriate
- Uncertainties, doubts, and fears
- Superstitions and rituals
- Sinning or doing something immoral
- Body and physical health
- Perfectionism
- Symmetry or order

Review this list and think about what theme your OCD represents. Some people have more than one concern, and your particular OCD worry may not be on this list. That's okay. Just try to categorize what issue bothers you the most. This reflection will help you complete the next exercise.

Starting with ten triggers

After identifying your particular OCD theme, make a list of ten situations that trigger your distress. Rate each trigger based on the *ugh factor* (the amount of distress an obsession or trigger makes you feel):

Rating	What It Means
0	No distress at all.
1	Very slight, almost nonexistent unease.
2	A small feeling of unease.
3	Mild distress.
4	Noticeable distress, enough to be completely aware of bad feelings.
5	Moderate distress.

Rating	What It Means
6	Significant distress; disturbing physical symptoms such as a rapid heartbeat, muscle tightness, or stomach upset.
7	Starting to interfere with normal functioning, high distress.
8	Feeling overwhelmed and close to panic.
9	Unable to function in a normal way; extreme distress.
10	Loss of control; an extreme level of panic.

Take time to think about your own OCD theme, triggers, and obsessions. On your list, try to include some triggers that are relatively minor and others that are more difficult.

To help you out, consider a couple examples. William suffers from OCD. His major worry is about becoming contaminated by germs from a variety of sources. He avoids being in close contact with people when he can and spends a lot of time thinking about the possibility of becoming sick. His compulsions include excessive sanitation, handwashing, and avoidance. Table 10-1 is his trigger list.

TABLE 10-1 William's OCD Trigger List with Ugh Factors

Trigger	Ugh Factor (0–10)
Taking my child to the doctor	8
Touching the doorknob of any restroom outside my house	10
Opening doors outside my house	5
Being close to a homeless person	9
Driving by a hospital or clinic	4
Taking out the trash (without wearing gloves)	7
Being inside in public when someone sneezes or coughs	10
Being outside in public when someone sneezes or coughs	4
Using public transportation (planes, trains, subways, or busses)	9
Being at home when someone in my family is sick	3

Stephanie's OCD revolves around uncertainty. She constantly worries about doing or not doing something that will cause harm to herself, her home, her children, her work, or just about any other responsibility she has. She compulsively spends hours every day checking and rechecking. Table 10-2 is Stephanie's trigger list.

Now, in Worksheet 10-1, make your list. Be specific and don't forget things that you simply avoid in order to manage your distress. You may need a couple of days to come up with a list of ten items — that's okay. Identifying your triggers and ranking them is one of the most important steps in ERP.

TABLE 10-2 Stephanie's OCD Trigger List with Ugh Factors

Trigger	Ugh Factor (0–10)
Worrying that I forgot to lock the doors and someone will break in	8
Worrying that I left the stove on and the house will burn down	10
Worrying that I left the water running and the house will flood	5
Feeling a bump while driving and worrying that I might have hit someone	9
Worrying that I could've made a mistake at work	4
Not being sure if I made someone mad	7
Worrying that I forgot my phone, keys, and tissues	10
Worrying that I didn't understand the directions on the map	4
Worrying that I'll forget to pick up my child at daycare on time	9
Worrying that I might forget an important appointment	6

WORKSHEET 10-1 My OCD Trigger List and Ugh Factors

Trigger	Ugh Factor (0–10)

Choosing your challenge

Making an exposure list may make you a bit anxious. That's actually good, because writing down your obsessions and triggers is actually a form of exposure.

TIP

If you're working with a therapist and you find this task too challenging, be sure to discuss your concerns and ask for help.

Now, take a few minutes to review Worksheet 10-1 and rank your triggers from the easiest to the hardest one to face. Pick one or two somewhere in the middle. If you're working on your own, start with an ugh factor of 3 or 4. If you feel brave and you're working with a therapist, go higher. Those will be your first ERP targets.

Here's what William and Stephanie, from the previous section, decide to work on:

- William's concern is contamination. He decides to start his exposure by opening doors using his hand and taking out the trash. He doesn't want to tackle opening restroom doors yet but agrees to try other doors. His decision to work on the trash relates to the constant hassle he experiences of putting on latex gloves and then washing his hands until they're raw.
- Stephanie is working with a therapist. She feels strongly that her routine of checking the house before work is the most important obsession to work on. Even though it ranks high on her list, the constant checking is making her late for work and annoying her family. She believes that she can manage the challenge.

How are you feeling at this point? Take a few minutes and write about the challenge you choose to start with in Worksheet 10-2.

WORKSHEET 10-2 My Reflections on the Challenge I've Chosen to Start With

REMEMBER

Your particular obsession may prevent you from performing real-life exposures. For example, if you obsess about the possibility of urinating or defecating in public, the exposure certainly wouldn't have you do that. Or if you have obsessions about being a sinner, you wouldn't be expected to purposely sin and see what happens. In these cases, you would imagine the exposure or try virtual reality (VR). Your therapist can help you develop these experiences.

Conducting Exposures and Collecting Data

Now is the time to start your ERP. Take a few deep breaths. Hold each breath for four seconds, and exhale slowly. Expect to experience some discomfort. ERP is hard work, and you must have at least some distress to learn from the experience. But the distress will be tolerable and won't last long. ERP is worth the investment because it can lead to long-lasting symptom reduction or even elimination.

WARNING

If you feel paralyzed with fear and can't face this process alone, seek help from a mental health professional.

During ERP, it's important to collect data. Doing so helps you understand the process and document your progress. The next sections tell you how. I use the examples of William and Stephanie to illustrate the process.

Starting exposure

When you start exposure, you want to be successful. So, take the trigger or obsession you decide to work on and break it down into manageable tasks, going from easy to hard.

Repeat the easiest exposure as many times as it takes for you to complete it with minimal distress. For example, William eventually wants to be able to open most doors using his bare hand. But he isn't ready to do that all at once. So, he determines something he can start with that doesn't seem impossible and gradually increases the difficulty. Here is his list:

1. I will use a tissue to open the door.
2. I will open a door with my hand as fast as possible.
3. I will hold a doorknob for 30 seconds.
4. I will hold a doorknob for one minute.

REMEMBER

A critical component of ERP is response prevention. In other words, you don't perform your normal compulsion. In William's case, he touches this doorknob without washing his hands immediately after.

Stephanie, who feels uncertain and repeatedly checks the stove, locks, and windows before she leaves, has a therapist who helps her slowly decrease her compulsive checking despite having the obsession that harm will come to her home and family. Normally, her checking routine takes at least an hour every morning. Here is her exposure list:

1. I will allow myself to check the stove, doors, and windows three times before I leave.
2. I will check only twice.
3. I will check only once.
4. I will not check at all.

TIP

Stephanie's case compulsive checking is the target behavior. The distress over not checking will decrease over time with ERP.

Break down your trigger into four manageable steps. Write them down in Worksheet 10-3.

WORKSHEET 10-3 Steps for Facing My Trigger

____

____

____

____

____

____

____

____

____

____

____

____

____

____

____

____

Tracking discomfort

To illustrate the process of tracking your discomfort, let's return to William, whose contamination fears keep him from touching doorknobs. In the previous section, he broke this down into several tasks. Next, he wrote each task in Table 10-3 and began his exposure while rating his ugh factor at the beginning, after several seconds, and after a minute. He went through each step until his distress started to decrease.

While doing these exposures, he didn't wash his hands even though he desperately wanted to. That's the response prevention part.

TABLE 10-3 William's Progress during ERP

Trigger	Ugh Factor (0–10)
Opening a door while holding a tissue	8, 10, 4
Opening a door with my hand as fast as possible	6, 4, 2
Holding a doorknob for 30 seconds	9, 10, 8
Holding a doorknob for one minute	10, 10, 9

William has some more work to do. He should continue to repeat these exercises until his ugh factor ratings are below 3. And then keep repeating them until his distress is very slight. Before he begins another challenge, he should be able to routinely open doors with his bare hands.

Stephanie's task is to decrease the time she spends compulsively checking. Every morning before work, she is sure that she leaves doors and windows open or unlocked and the stove on full blast. She repeatedly checks and rechecks, keeping her from getting to work on time. Table 10-4 shows her ratings during initial exposures.

TABLE 10-4 Stephanie's Progress during ERP

Trigger	Ugh Factor (0–10)
Checking the stove, doors, and windows only three times before leaving the house	6, 8, 2
Checking the stove, doors, and windows only twice before leaving the house	8, 8, 6
Checking the stove, doors, and windows only once before leaving the house	9, 10, 8
Not checking the stove, doors, and windows at all before leaving the house	10, 10, 10

Like William, Stephanie has much more work to do. With her therapist, she devises more exposures. Her therapist may even refer Stephanie to work through some of her thinking errors (see Part 4) in addition to continuing guided ERP.

At this point, you've picked your trigger and you're ready to begin. If your trigger involves touching something, go ahead and do it and then do it again. You may resist rechecking something or not saying a certain phrase. If it's thinking a shameful thought, go for it.

Stay with the trigger. In Worksheet 10-4, rate how much distress you feel by using the ugh factor scale at the beginning of the exposure and after a few seconds. Keep measuring it until it starts to come down. Believe me, with time, your distress will decrease. Don't try to suppress any obsessive thoughts or fears. Notice them. They're just thoughts. Let them be, even if they frighten you. It's important to experience your fears during the exposure.

WORKSHEET 10-4 Checking Your Progress during ERP

Trigger	Ugh Factor

Repeating the process until your ugh factor is manageable

You may be thinking that exposure was pretty easy to complete. You managed to stay on a task for a minute or so and you're ready to celebrate. Not so fast. In order to let ERP do its job, you need to step it up a bit. Stay with the trigger for a full ten minutes or so. Repeat multiple times a week. For learning to occur, you must feel the feelings of fear, distress, and uncertainty.

Then after multiple times, your brain starts to learn that touching a garbage can didn't make you sick, not rechecking the locks for the sixth time didn't invite the burglars in, and changing your routines didn't lead to catastrophe.

When your brain begins to understand that your obsessions may not be accurate, learning and retraining start to occur. But you're not done yet.

Climbing the Hierarchy

Success breeds confidence. Hopefully, your beginning exposures gave you the courage to move ahead. Go back to Worksheet 10-1 and choose some challenges that are more difficult. Repeat the steps in the "Conducting Exposures and Collecting Data" section, earlier in this chapter, until your distress begins to decline significantly.

TIP

Make sure that you practice your exposures in more than one setting. For example, if you can't stand to touch doorknobs, make sure you touch lots of doorknobs — in your house, in your therapist's office, in the mall, at a restaurant, and so on.

Think of yourself as an investigative journalist. ERP is your story. Ask yourself: Did you manage to complete your ERP? Did your fear decrease over time? Did you learn anything new through your experience?

Stopping when you're tired

Some days are better than others. If you're sick or tired, skip a day. Don't worry about repeating exposures when you're weary. However, if you find yourself making excuses, such as "I just don't feel like it today," that could mean that you're trying to avoid facing your fear. Consider talking to your therapist or finding one if you don't have one already.

Feeling free to repeat

As you face more and more of your obsessions and delay your compulsions, go back and repeat some of the ERP exercises that you were successful at doing. This will remind you of your progress and reinforce your earlier learning.

Also, when you're feeling discouraged about your progress, repeating earlier, successful exposures can boost your confidence in the process. I encourage you to have a bit of fun. I know that sounds counterintuitive, but doing ERP can be quite entertaining. Looking back on situations that once caused you distress can lighten your mood and make you realize how far you've come.

Continuing until you're comfortable

Keep practicing all your exposures until you feel very small amounts of distress. Some people find their ugh factor reaching 0 in some situations. However, you should expect occasional bouts of discomfort regarding the same or even different triggers.

Use your knowledge of the process of ERP to handle those temporary setbacks. They're more likely to recur when you have more stress in your life or you're sick or fatigued.

TIP

The knowledge you gain doing ERP can be applied to many other real-life challenges. When faced with an unknown obstacle, breaking things down into small doable steps, not allowing negative thoughts to prevent you from trying, and being persistent all help you jump over hurdles.

In Worksheet 10-5, take some notes about your experiences with ERP. Were you successful? Do you have any questions you'd like to talk to your therapist about?

WORKSHEET 10-5 My Reflections on ERP

Troubleshooting Exposure and Response Prevention

ERP involves deliberately confronting your obsessive triggers while resisting the urge to perform compulsive acts to relieve your distress. Basically, the brain gets used to the distress and eventually the distress decreases.

REMEMBER

Habituation refers to the process of getting used to a stimulus over time. It's a common form of learning. For example, if you visit New York City, you may be kept awake by the constant noise of trucks, sirens, and people. But if you live there, you hardly notice it. Exposure therapy involves the same principle: Over time and with repetition, a distressing obsession becomes less noticeable.

Sometimes, ERP gets stuck or doesn't appear to work at all. The science behind ERP is solid. It should work. But roadblocks, either intentional or unintentional, can hinder learning.

Distraction and dissociation

When people experience trauma, one method of protecting themselves is through a process called *dissociation*. Dissociation involves disconnecting emotionally from what's going on. It's a way of stepping back from the trauma, and it disrupts memory, perception, and consciousness.

For example, dissociation can happen when someone is being physically or sexually abused. They often report feeling out of their body, looking down from afar. This especially occurs when the abuse is chronic.

Dissociation can be an adaptive response to an intense trauma; however, it can also block the benefits of ERP. During ERP, you must actively engage with the process.

Another way to avoid the distress of ERP is to become distracted. It's not a great idea to be looking at your phone while engaging in ERP. Again, staying fully aware during the process is the goal and the way forward during exposures.

WARNING

Although some medications are considered good treatments for OCD, others can prevent the emotional distress needed for ERP to work effectively. Talk to your prescribing doctor about which medications are appropriate and see Chapter 15 for more about medications and OCD.

Reassurance seeking

Another strategy people often use during ERP is asking others for more help than they really need or asking others if everything will be okay. Reassurance seeking is often part of the OCD worry cycle. If you have someone helping you with ERP, tell them at the start not to offer safety messages.

REMEMBER

Reassurance seeking can be a compulsive checking behavior. It temporarily reduces distress but quickly leads to more compulsive checking.

Taking on too much

Some people try to start working on their OCD with so much enthusiasm that they try too hard to cover everything all at once. It's critical to go low and slow — make sure you don't experience too much distress, and start the exposures slowly. Moving too fast doesn't give the brain a chance to learn and rewire. And taking on too much emotional discomfort discourages repeated exposures.

TIP

As you progress through ERP, take the time to pat yourself on the back. ERP requires persistence and dedication. Reward yourself with a treat as you move forward in your recovery.

Do you have any acts or behaviors that interfere with ERP? Write about them in Worksheet 10-6 and talk to your therapist about them. Also plan to reward yourself for progress. Great work!

WORKSHEET 10-6 Thinking about My Behaviors That Interfere with ERP

4

Clearing Up Obsessional Thinking

IN THIS PART . . .

Check out how uncertainty plagues the minds of those with obsessive-compulsive disorder (OCD).

Keep track of realistic risks of living.

Take a look at how thoughts, feelings, and behaviors interact.

Deal with distorted thoughts.

Improve your skills for handling stress.

IN THIS CHAPTER

» Getting comfortable with uncertainty

» Smelling the roses today

» Understanding risk

Chapter 11
Detailing the Doubting Disorder

Are you pretty sure the sun will come up tomorrow? Probably. However, scientists predict that the chances of a civilization ending collision with an asteroid are about 1 in 10,000. Interestingly, that's about the same risk of being injured by a toilet or finding a four-leaf clover.

Most people don't spend too much time worrying about toilet injuries, asteroid collisions, or finding a four-leaf clover. But for people with obsessive-compulsive disorder (OCD), statistical facts and figures are meaningless. They spend hours worrying about things that rarely happen.

For example, the chance of being contaminated by touching something in a public restroom is basically just above zero (certainly less than the chance of being hit by an asteroid). Most illnesses require direct, fresh contact. And hard surfaces don't allow long-term survival of bacteria or viruses. Washing hands once after using a restroom is the best way to prevent the low risk of catching something. And if your immune system is compromised, consider using a paper towel for turning off the water.

Celebrating Uncertainty

OCD is often called the doubting disease. The OCD brain concocts stories of uncertainty. And if you think about life, nothing is absolutely certain. Many people claim that nothing is certain except death and taxes. But you never really know. There're probably a lot of tax cheats out there who never file. And some people believe in everlasting life, others believe in a continuance through legacy and memory, and some believe in reincarnation. That shoots down the certainty of death and taxes.

Uncertainty leaves people with OCD feeling anxious and distressed. Here are some of the common uncertainties people with OCD worry about:

- Did I write this perfectly?
- Did I make a horrible mistake?
- What if my phone is causing me cancer?
- Did I lock the door?
- Did I hit someone with my car and not remember it?
- Did I sin?
- What if I hurt my children?
- Am I really alive at all?
- What if I left the coffee pot on?
- What is the true meaning of life?
- Is my counter really clean?

What are you uncertain about? How certain are you that your worries are likely to occur? Put your thoughts in Worksheet 11-1.

Challenging uncertainty

Life is chaotic, unknowable, and unpredictable. Uncertainty is a constant part of life. If you stay worried about what might happen, you can't fully engage in the opportunities to live fully. Your quest for certainty is impossible. Instead of trying to establish certainty, challenge the very concept of it.

Embracing uncertainty

Some of life's challenges you have quite a bit of control over. For example, if you eat right, exercise, and have a network of people you care about, you've got a pretty good chance of being healthy. But something bad could always happen. You might get struck by lightning or an asteroid. You can't do much about that.

WORKSHEET 11-1 My Reflections on Uncertainty

Understand that you may have influence over outcomes, but at no time do you have complete control. Some things are entirely out of your control. For example, you don't have control over the economy, traffic, other people, history, or the weather.

REMEMBER

You do have considerable control over your thoughts, your behaviors, and your interpretations of events. And changing thoughts, behaviors, and attitudes impact your feelings.

What ifs and the present moment

OCD generates anxious and hypothetical "what ifs." Those hypothetical possibilities are unhelpful and usually produce negative predictions that rarely happen. Staying stranded in "what ifs" keeps people stuck in the past and future and robs them from living in the present. Here are some typical OCD what ifs:

- What if I chose the wrong relationship?
- What if I hurt someone in the past?
- What if I never get clean enough?
- What if I don't save enough for the future?

» What if I harm my family?

» What if I'm a sinner?

TIP

Instead of living in the past and future, stay present in the moment. Stay in the here and now, where life is really happening. Focus on your surroundings. What do you see? What can you control?

REMEMBER

What ifs are only thoughts and not actual accurate predictions or reflections of reality. Concentrate on what you can do, now, today. Turn to Chapters 13 and 14 for more strategies on living in the present moment.

Do you generate what ifs and demands for certainty? Do you have thoughts about challenging those desires and living in the present moment? Reflect on those thoughts in Worksheet 11-2.

WORKSHEET 11-2 My Reflections on What Ifs

Risky Living

Living life is a risky business. Many dangerous situations present themselves regularly. People have to cross streets, climb stairs, and negotiate traffic. Other people live in war zones, or areas in which natural disasters may occur. We're all exposed to dangerous chemicals, viruses, and bacteria. No wonder people worry. There are good reasons to be on guard. But most people understand risk and still experience large portions of time during which they don't worry. They live their lives fully despite knowing there is always a possibility of disaster.

Not so for people with OCD. They worry about danger to the point of being miserable most of the time. Many of the risks that plague those with OCD are extremely remote possibilities. They're very unlikely to occur. They're imagined risks, not based on direct evidence. And quite a few OCD worries make very little sense.

Exaggerated risk

People with OCD tend to inflate not only the possibility of risk but the degree of suffering that's likely to occur. The OCD mind doesn't respond rationally but magnifies the possible consequences of their irrational fears. Each small risk becomes the worst case possible. They believe that the only response for the OCD mind is to complete the associated compulsion, promising fleeting, temporary relief from the fear.

Do you exaggerate the risk of something occurring? Write about it in Worksheet 11-3.

WORKSHEET 11-3 My Reflections on Exaggerated Risk

Depending on your particular OCD theme, you may have different catastrophic fears. For example, someone who has relationship OCD may worry all the time that their partner will leave them; they may believe if that happens, they'll basically crumble up and die, unable to live alone. Someone with contamination OCD may be certain that if the bleach they used wasn't strong enough, they'll certainly become sick and die. And someone with checking OCD may be sure that the stove is leaking gas and if they don't get up to check, the house will explode. These fears feel very real and lead to great suffering.

You can challenge exaggerated beliefs by using direct experiences, logic, and common sense. If you tend to exaggerate the risk of something horrendous happening, complete the exercise in Worksheet 11-4.

WORKSHEET 11-4 Ending Exaggerated Risk

Question	Answer
Are your worries based on information from your senses (smell, taste, touch, sight, or sound)?	
Do you have evidence that your concern is not necessarily accurate, but it keeps returning to your mind?	
Do other people share your concern and see your worries as logical?	
Is there anything at all that would change your mind about your worry?	
After answering these questions, do your beliefs about risk change?	

TIP

Realistic risks are supported by direct evidence. OCD exaggerates risk. If you need more help in challenging these beliefs, turn to Chapters 12 and 13.

THE COVID-19 PANDEMIC AND OCD

At the beginning of the COVID-19 pandemic, you probably had the experience of contamination OCD. In the early days, many people were afraid to leave their homes. Touching doorknobs became something to avoid. People shoved the door open with covered hands or elbows and immediately used hand sanitizer. For a while, the public was advised to rinse and disinfect their groceries. The economy shut down. As months went by and cases skyrocketed, there was a parallel epidemic of doubt, uncertainty, and distress.

The mental health of the population suffered during the pandemic. Symptoms of anxiety, depression, and trauma-related disorders were reported in over a third of adults. Substance abuse increased. By the following year, more than 40 percent of the population was either anxious or depressed. Teens and young adults suffered even more, with an astonishing 25 percent of that age group reporting suicidal thoughts. Even though many people stayed clear of emergency rooms because of fear of exposure, mental health visits during the pandemic increased.

If you had OCD during the pandemic, things were much worse. Those with contamination-related OCD reported an extreme worsening of symptoms, especially during periods of enforced isolation. Those with mild and moderate OCD became worse, and those who had been in remission from OCD tended to relapse.

Although it seems like the pandemic was a lifetime ago, for many people the stress and related mental health problems linger.

Overinflated personal responsibility

People with OCD, especially those who fear that they may harm others, tend to believe that their own power somehow keeps themselves and other people safe. In addition, if something bad does happen, they feel responsible for the negative outcomes.

These powers may be compulsive actions, superstitious behaviors, or avoidance. The actions tend to be centered around issues such as safety, perfectionism, guilt, and social relationships. Here are a few examples:

- I dropped a staple on the floor. I have to find it or an animal or child will eat it and die.
- If I don't keep my house sanitized, everyone will get sick and it will all be because of me.
- If this work product isn't perfect, the whole team will be fired, so I must check and recheck my work.
- I shouldn't flush the toilet so much because the future of the world's water is in my hands.
- I could inadvertently insult someone, so I should apologize before I say anything.
- If I don't recheck the lock 14 times, my home will be burglarized.
- If I go to the same restaurant as I did on the day an airplane crashed, another plane will crash.
- My partner is in a bad mood. It's always my fault. I need to fix it and ask what I did wrong.
- I feel guilty when others make mistakes because I should've done more to help.
- I need to go back over my steps several times to make sure I didn't track any dirt into the house. If I miss even a speck of dirt, the house will be contaminated.

Having inflated responsibility is common in people with OCD. Do you have beliefs that you have control over or power to cause or prevent any negative outcomes in your life or the lives of others? How certain are you that those thoughts are accurate? Reflect on those thoughts in Worksheet 11-5.

TIP

If you have OCD, you may believe that you truly are responsible for many or most negative outcomes. Answer the questions in Worksheet 11-6.

TIP

If you're having trouble with this exercise, talk it over with your therapist or a trusted friend or family member.

The final fear: Death

Obsessions about death are common in people with OCD. In fact, those with OCD who have death anxiety tend to have the most severe cases of OCD. Their lives are likely to be consumed with obsessions and compulsions that interfere with their ability to carry on their daily responsibilities.

WORKSHEET 11-5 My Reflections on Inflated Responsibility

WORKSHEET 11-6 Decreasing Inflated Personal Responsibility

Question	Answer
How responsible do you currently feel for the potential negative outcome?	
Are there other possible reasons such as the neighborhood, other people, biological issues, accidents, social issues, or psychological problems that could have any impact?	
Is it possible that the negative outcome was random bad luck?	
If you asked a friend how much responsibility for the negative outcome they would attribute to you, what would they likely say?	
After answering these questions, has your belief about your relative responsibility changed? If so, how?	

Fears about death are often related to trauma — either witnessing trauma or experiencing trauma. In addition, those with contamination OCD are especially prone to having death anxiety. In addition, fear of death is also associated with people whose OCD revolves around religious content, sexual deviancy, or aggressive actions. Fear of death is also associated with a higher risk of suicide.

WARNING

If your obsessions and compulsions revolve around death anxiety, I strongly advise you to seek professional help.

If fear of death is the topic of some of your obsessions and compulsions, answer the questions in Worksheet 11-7. Take your time and think about your responses and answer as best you can.

WORKSHEET 11-7 Examining Fear of Death

Question	Answer
Are you afraid of dying?	
Are you afraid of leaving loved ones behind?	
Are you afraid of leaving unfinished business?	
Are you afraid of the afterlife or the unknown?	
What do you do to quell your fears?	
How much time is consumed by your obsessions and compulsions regarding death?	
What symptoms do you experience when you have the fear?	
Have you ever witnessed a death or a traumatic event?	
Have you experienced a trauma?	
Does your fear of death prevent you from living a full and meaningful life?	

TIP

After answering these questions, you may want to talk to your therapist. Because fear of death is a relatively common component of OCD, exposure and response prevention (ERP) is still considered the gold standard treatment. However, other treatments, such as those described in Chapters 12, 13, and 14, may be implemented when exposures are too difficult or not appropriate.

In Worksheet 11-8, take a few moments to write about your thoughts and feelings after reading about risk, fear, and death anxiety.

WORKSHEET 11-8 My Reflections on Fear of Death

IN THIS CHAPTER

- **Finding out that thoughts are just thoughts**
- **Recording thoughts and interpretations**
- **Testing out thoughts**
- **Rethinking thoughts**

Chapter 12 Debriefing Distortions

Cognitive therapy is based on the premise that the way you interpret events influences your emotional response and how you behave. Put simply, what you think about something largely determines your feelings. It helps you understand the connections between your thoughts, feelings, and behaviors. Cognitive therapy is one of the evidence-based treatments for obsessive-compulsive disorder (OCD).

In this chapter, I detail the common thoughts and distortions that get in the way of feeling good and meeting goals and obligations. A practical way to think about cognitive therapy is the catch, check, and change method:

1. **Catch.** Become aware of your thoughts.
2. **Check.** Discover ways to examine your thoughts for possible distortions.
3. **Change.** Replace your distorted thought with a more balanced, reasonable thought.

Meeting the Common Thought Distortions

Thought distortions are ways your mind distorts information you're getting from your environment. For example, some people are generally optimistic, and others are generally pessimistic. Let's say the stock market goes down significantly one day. An optimist might think, "Oh well, it's just a temporary setback, it'll go back up again." A pessimist might think, "There goes my future retirement. I'll never recover and I'll certainly end up in the poorhouse."

The same event, two very different interpretations. The optimist probably feels pretty good and doesn't really think any more about the stock market. But the pessimist feels panicked and may even make some bad decisions about what to do with their money.

Thought distortions are common exaggerated interpretations of events that tend to cause people to misinterpret reality. They're mental habits that can lead to negative emotions such as anxiety or depression. Distortions are foundational in OCD thinking. Here are the most common types of distorted thinking:

- **Black-and-white thinking:** This common pattern of distorted thinking divides all incidents, events, or characteristics in one or the other extreme way. Someone is totally good or completely evil. There are no nuances. A person who worries about the possibility of sinning may believe that if they have one weird thought, they're horrible sinners and certainly going to burn in hell. Someone whose OCD centers around perfectionism believes that a small, almost invisible error means complete ruin. There are no shades of gray, only black and white.
- **Dismissing evidence:** People with OCD often dismiss evidence that their obsessive worries may not be entirely true. Any possible information that their fears are not absolutely accurate is simply disregarded. Because there is always a tiny possible danger in their mind, they believe that they must continue with compulsive checking, cleaning, avoiding, or ritualizing to protect themselves or others. No amount of explanation or logical evidence works to relieve them of the abundance of doubt that remains in the OCD mind.
- **Overgeneralizing:** The thought distortion of overgeneralization involves taking one fleeting bit of information and applying it to just about everything. For example, if someone has the intrusive thought, "I might be contaminated," they may believe that from that point on, they must wash constantly and clean compulsively; they never believe that their rituals are enough to cleanse themselves permanently. Similarly, someone whose concern is about potentially harming others may believe that a random obsession concerning driving their car into a crowd certainly means that they will eventually do that action. A person who is obsessively concerned about a close relationship may misinterpret a bland expression in their partner as evidence of disdain.
- **Emotional reasoning:** This distortion prevails throughout the population of people with and without mental health issues. Emotional reasoning occurs when someone feels something and believes that their feelings indicate some truth. Feelings are not facts. During emotional reasoning, for example, if you're sad, you believe there must be something real to be sad about. If you're fearful, the world must be dangerous and scary. If you're ashamed or you feel guilty, you must have done something wrong.

  You can easily see how people with OCD use emotional reasoning. When their obsessions lead to feelings of distress, they believe that the distress means that their obsessions must be true. Therefore, they perform their ritualistic responses (cleaning, checking, avoiding, or another ritual). Thus, they remain stuck in the cycle of obsession, distress, compulsion, followed by temporary relief.

REMEMBER

Feelings are never wrong, but just because you feel something doesn't make it true. Feelings can be inaccurate messengers. Emotional reasoning detours around facts, bypasses logic, and causes unnecessary suffering.

- **Thought-action fusion:** Thought-action fusion is the belief that just the act of thinking about something means that it must be true. For example, if someone has a weird immoral thought that they might be a child abuser, they think that means it's true. Or if someone has the thought that they might drive their car into a group of people, they think it will actually occur. Someone with contamination OCD might think that something is dirty, so it must be true.

REMEMBER

Bizarre and weird thoughts happen to everyone once in a while. People with thought-action fusion distortions believe that their thoughts are always true and will lead to action.

- **Unreliable forecasting:** Unreliable forecasting is looking into the future and believing something will happen without any evidence. Some people use this distortion to paint a rosy picture of their future despite being in jail for life, having a terrible terminal illness, or being recklessly stupid about planning for their later years. But most people use unreliable forecasting to predict doom and gloom without much evidence. For example, someone with contamination OCD might predict that if they don't clean all the surfaces of the kitchens and bathrooms with bleach several times a day, they and their family will certainly succumb to a vicious virus. Or someone with just right OCD may predict that a single mistake or typo will cause them to lose their job.
- **Mind reading:** As with most thought distortions, mind reading is commonly used by everyone from time to time. Mind reading is simply believing that you know what others are thinking. Unfortunately, even the best-trained psychologist is unable to fully understand or get into someone else's head. Mind reading becomes a problem when it's biased, usually to the negative, and when people believe in the worst-case scenario. You might see someone with a neutral facial expression and believe they're angry. If your friend replies to your text with just a quick response, you might see it as a rejection. Also, someone with OCD who worries about shameful thoughts and obsessions might falsely believe that others can read their minds, increasing their guilt and shame.
- **Catastrophizing:** Like unreliable forecasting, catastrophizers look at the future without sufficient evidence and make predictions. However, in this case, the mind magnifies the horribleness of some small possibility and exaggerates the possible outcomes. For example, you get a paper cut; it hurts, and you imagine that it will most probably become infected and even possibly lead to sepsis, amputation, or death. That may be a bit of an exaggeration of catastrophizing, but you get the idea. Catastrophizing is a common thought distortion among people with OCD.

In Worksheet 12-1, write about the thought distortions that commonly impact your thinking. It's perfectly normal to engage in thought distortions, what's important is to recognize them.

WORKSHEET 12-1 My Thought Distortions

____

____

____

____

____

____

____

____

____

____

____

____

____

____

____

____

____

____

Catching the Culprits: Thought Trackers

Thought distortions warp your perceptions of the real world. If you have OCD, you're likely to be influenced by these misperceptions of reality. Figuring out which distortions are getting in your way is the first step in understanding how your thoughts influence your feelings. After you become aware of your usual culprits, change is possible. In order to track which distortions are causing you problems, the following exercise helps. Before you try one, here are a couple of examples to help you better understand the concepts.

Joey has what is commonly called "hit-and-run OCD." A person with this obsession firmly believes that they've hit someone with their car. Joey often stops, gets out of the car, looks around, and checks. After returning to the car, he may go forward only a bit then return to the supposed scene. This pattern can sometimes happen over a period of multiple hours. You can imagine how difficult that could make Joey's life. Table 12-1 shows what a thought tracker might look like for Joey.

TABLE 12-1 Joey's Thought Tracker

Event	Thoughts and Feelings	Thought Distortion
Driving out of the driveway, I felt a bit of a bump.	I didn't check the mirror enough times. There might've been a child behind me. I probably hit them. I'm a horrible person, a murderer. I'll spend my life in jail.	Unreliable forecasting Dismissing evidence Thought-action fusion Catastrophizing
I'm on a highway and the traffic is congested. There's an accident on the side of the road.	I surely caused that accident on the side of the road. I'm a terrible driver. I feel horrible, so it must've been me.	Black-and-white thinking Emotional reasoning Thought-action fusion Unreliable forecasting Dismissing evidence

You can see that Joey doesn't have any evidence that he hit someone or caused an accident. He believes that he knows the outcome, again without evidence. He uses black-and-white thinking to label himself horrible, and because his emotions are negative, Joey believes that he must be guilty and he's sure that he'll end up in jail.

Before you complete your own thought tracker, see if you can identify the distorted thoughts in Worksheet 12-2. Circle the distortions you think apply.

WORKSHEET 12-2 Thought Tracker Practice

Event	Thoughts and Feelings	Thought Distortion
Walking by a group of homeless people	Those people have bugs that could infect me. I'll probably get extremely sick and possibly die. I feel stressed, so I must be sick. I need to go home immediately and throw my contaminated clothes in the garbage and take a long shower.	Black-and-white thinking Dismissing evidence Overgeneralizing Emotional reasoning Thought-action fusion Unreliable forecasting Mind reading Catastrophizing
Seeing a mistake on a text just after sending it out	That's horrible. The person getting this text is going to think I'm an idiot. I could lose my job over this mistake. I feel so ashamed, which proves that I'm going to get fired.	Black-and-white thinking Dismissing evidence Overgeneralizing Emotional reasoning Thought-action fusion Unreliable forecasting Mind reading Catastrophizing

(continued)

WORKSHEET 12-2 ***(continued)***

Event	Thoughts and Feelings	Thought Distortion
Needing to cook a meal for my family and chop up vegetables	I might lose control and not be able to stop myself from stabbing my family. I'm not safe around sharp objects. How can I be 100 percent certain that I'm not a killer? Because I have these thoughts, they must be true. I feel horrible and guilty already. My family must think I'm crazy. I guess I'll order a pizza.	Black-and-white thinking Dismissing evidence Overgeneralizing Emotional reasoning Thought-action fusion Unreliable forecasting Mind reading Catastrophizing

You can see a variety of thought distortions among these examples. There are overlaps and no completely right or wrong answers. Everyone has different interpretations. Don't stress about being perfect!

Now it's time for you to complete your own thought tracker in Worksheet 12-3. Ask yourself what was going on when you noticed OCD obsessions and compulsions becoming more prevalent. Then summarize that event in the first column. In the second column, describe your thoughts and feelings. Finally, in the third column circle any of the thought distortions that may be occurring.

WORKSHEET 12-3 My Thought Tracker

Event	Thoughts and Feelings	Thought Distortion
		Black-and-white thinking Dismissing evidence Overgeneralizing Emotional reasoning Thought-action fusion Unreliable forecasting Mind reading Catastrophizing
		Black-and-white thinking Dismissing evidence Overgeneralizing Emotional reasoning Thought-action fusion Unreliable forecasting Mind reading Catastrophizing

Event	Thoughts and Feelings	Thought Distortion
		Black-and-white thinking
		Dismissing evidence
		Overgeneralizing
		Emotional reasoning
		Thought-action fusion
		Unreliable forecasting
		Mind reading
		Catastrophizing

TIP

If you have difficulty with this exercise, be sure to talk it over with your therapist.

Challenging the Distortions

When you're able to identify your distorted thoughts, it's time to challenge them. There are multiple techniques for doing this. In this section, I offer some of the more common ones used in cognitive therapy today.

TIP

If you're working with a therapist, be sure to discuss your thought distortions with them and ask for help in challenging them together. Cognitive therapists help you practice more realistic, adaptive, and beneficial thinking.

Examining evidence

This technique involves taking a thought and checking the evidence for and against it. It's often used during exposure and response prevention (ERP). This additional strategy requires considering a thought as a hypothesis rather than the absolute truth. Then you ask yourself questions to see if there is evidence to support or dispute the thought. Common questions include the following:

- What evidence do I have that supports this thought?
- Is there any evidence that refutes this thought?
- Is this thought illogical or distorted in any way?
- Is this thought based on how I feel, or is it based on fact?
- Have I ever tested out this thought?
- Are there any times in my life that this thought isn't true?
- How horrible would the consequences of giving up this thought be?
- Is this thought helping me lead a better life?

To clarify, here's an example of Sailor, who has an obsession regarding symmetry. Her home has to have a certain order or she feels horrible. She can't really describe the unease of things being out of place, but she feels that she has no control over her obsession and compulsive ordering. The list of tasks takes many hours of her day. Here are just a few of the numerous demands of her obsession:

- The remote must be placed perfectly centered on the coffee table.
- The pillows must be arranged in the correct order on the couch.
- The pictures on the wall must be perfectly straight.
- The carpet fringe must be perfectly straight.

Let's see how Sailor may respond to some of the questions examining the evidence. Table 12-2 shows her responses.

TABLE 12-2 Sailor's Examination of the Evidence That Her House Must Be in Perfect Order

Question	Answer
What evidence do I have that supports this thought?	I'm not sure, but I really believe that it's true.
Is there any evidence that refutes this thought?	I've seen other homes out of order, and it doesn't really bother me that much.
Is this thought illogical or distorted in any way?	Not to me. But I guess my friends and family think I'm too obsessed.
Is this thought based on how I feel, or is it based on fact?	I see now that this is based on how I feel.
Have I ever tested out this thought?	Once when I had the flu, I wasn't able to do everything. I was so sick, I didn't care. But then when I got better, I went right back to the compulsions.
Are there any times in my life when this thought isn't true?	When I'm traveling, I don't really think about it too much.
How horrible would the consequences of giving up this thought be?	I would feel out of sorts and probably miserable most of the time.
Is this thought helping me lead a better life?	This one got me. No, I spend way too much time straightening, and it takes away time from my family. I also tend to get very crabby when someone messes up my stuff.

Examining the evidence is one of many good techniques that can support treating OCD. Now that you've seen how it works, complete Worksheet 12-4 to see how your own obsessive thought holds up to scrutiny.

WORKSHEET 12-4 My Examination of the Evidence

Question	Answer
What evidence do I have that supports this thought?	
Is there any evidence that refutes this thought?	
Is this thought illogical or distorted in any way?	
Is this thought based on how I feel, or is it based on fact?	
Have I ever tested out this thought?	
Are there any times in my life when this thought isn't true?	
How horrible would the consequences of giving up this thought be?	
Is this thought helping me lead a better life?	

Decoupling thoughts and feelings

Many people find it difficult to separate their thoughts from their feelings. To help you separate the two, observe your thoughts as simply mental events. Try to identify the difference between having a thought and feeling a feeling. Label your thoughts as thoughts. This helps to put distance between your thoughts and feelings.

TIP

For example, you feel filthy after having to ride public transportation. Your mind becomes filled with obsessions about contamination. Instead of saying to yourself, "I'm infected and contaminated," say "I'm having the thought that I'm contaminated."

Because of an overactive alarm system, people with OCD often sound a fire alarm when there is only a spark or a wisp of harmless smoke. They use emotional reasoning to believe that every feeling they have must be a true reflection of reality.

Try to remind yourself that just because you feel dread, fear, shame, contaminated, or uneasy, that doesn't mean that there is actually something happening to cause these feelings. Feel your feeling, but don't take it too seriously. Go back and examine the evidence.

REMEMBER

Just because you feel something, doesn't make it true. And just because you think something, doesn't make it true. Examine the evidence.

Taking a broader perspective

What seems to be a catastrophe or horrendous event today may have little importance later in your life. People generally overestimate the impact of events. In the moment, OCD distress probably feels overwhelming. Here are some common feelings and beliefs people with OCD have:

- I can't tolerate this anxiety.
- If I stop repeating words in the right order, bad things will certainly happen.
- I can't stand to make mistakes. I must check and recheck until everything is perfect.
- I feel so ashamed about my crazy thoughts, I believe I'm damned to hell.
- If I don't disinfect this thing, I might cause my family to get sick.

Hopefully, you're getting treatment for your OCD, and those sorts of thoughts will decrease in frequency. Ask yourself how sure you are that those thoughts will still impact you in the future. How about in a month or a year?

TIP

By stepping away from your current thoughts and feelings, you can put a little distance between the hurt of today and the reality of the future.

Being a friend to yourself

In addition to checking the evidence, separating thoughts from feelings, and stepping back, try giving yourself advice as if you were your own cherished friend. If your friend had the same thoughts and feelings that you did, what would you say to them? What kind of advice would you share? Take a few minutes and write a short note to yourself. Be kind.

Table 12-3 is an example of note to help you get started.

TABLE 12-3 An Example Letter

Dear friend, I understand you're worried about the possibility that you might soil yourself in public. That must really bother you a lot. I would be concerned about that, too. What do you think would happen if you actually did? I know if someone around me soiled themselves, I would feel sorry for them and do everything I could to help them get some privacy. I'd even help them get to their car or perhaps to a restroom to clean up. I would never judge someone who had an accident like that. No one would feel that the person was guilty or shameful. In fact, I would be concerned about their well-being. By the way, just checking, have you ever soiled yourself in public? What makes you believe that you might do that? Do you have any evidence at all? Well, that's all for now. I hope this helps. I really want you to be less stressed. I care about you. Your friend, Me

How do you think that person might feel after reading this letter to themselves? Better. Worksheet 12-5 is your turn to try this out. ***Remember:*** Be a supportive friend.

WORKSHEET 12-5 A Letter to Myself

Dear Me,

TIP

If you find this exercise to be helpful, save the letter to yourself and reread it when you feel a bit distressed by your OCD.

Reframing and replacing distorted thoughts

Throughout this chapter, I describe various techniques for challenging distorted thoughts. After you've identified your distorted thoughts, you can examine the evidence, separate thoughts from feelings, take a broader point of view, and be a friend to yourself.

Now, go back to the original thought tracker that you completed in Worksheet 12-3. If you haven't completed that worksheet, you can either review it or try this exercise on your own. Hopefully, you have some techniques that will help you rewrite your original thoughts and interpretations with new balanced ones. First, Table 12-4 provides an example for you to consider.

TABLE 12-4 Thought Tracker Example

Event	Thoughts and Feelings	New Balanced Thought
Walking by a group of homeless people	Those people have bugs that could infect me. I'll probably get extremely sick and possibly die. I feel stressed, so I must be sick. I need to go home immediately and throw my contaminated clothes in the garbage and take a long shower.	I might feel contaminated, but I have no evidence to support that. I know it makes me uncomfortable, but I can handle this feeling without throwing away my clothes and taking a shower. When I get home, it's okay to wash up and then get on with my day.
Seeing a mistake on a text just after sending it out	That's horrible. The person getting this text is going to think I'm an idiot. I could lose my job over this mistake. I feel so ashamed, which proves that I'm going to get fired.	I've never been fired or even scolded for making a minor error. I'm valued at work. Everyone makes mistakes from time to time.
I need to cook a meal for my family. I have to chop up vegetables.	I might lose control and not be able to stop myself from stabbing my family. I'm not safe around sharp objects. How can I be 100 percent certain that I'm not a killer? Because I have these thoughts, they must be true. I feel horrible and guilty already. My family must think I'm crazy. I guess I'll order a pizza.	I've used knives before. Even though I have these silly thoughts, I've never lost control and hurt anyone in my whole life. I would never hurt my family. These are just thoughts and not actually true. My negative feelings are reactions to untrue thoughts.

Worksheet 12-6 is your chance to give this a try on your own. Take your time. You might refer to various sections of this chapter to give you some ideas.

REMEMBER

If you get stuck on any exercise, be sure to share it with your therapist. If you decide to do this on your own, your therapist will love to see the results. Good luck!

WORKSHEET 12-6 My New Thought Tracker

Event	Thoughts and Feelings	New Balanced Thought

After completing this exercise, how do you feel? Are your new balanced thoughts based on evidence that you can see, feel, touch, or hear? Have your feelings changed as a result of new more balanced thinking? I hope so.

IN THIS CHAPTER

» Searching for peace

» Getting through tough times

» Playing the cards you're dealt

Chapter 13
Building Distress Tolerance

If you have obsessive-compulsive disorder (OCD), your life has likely been filled with worry, anxiety, and stress. In fact, if you're human, you've probably had your share of chaos, uncertainty, loss, and negative emotions. Sometimes those emotions become overwhelming.

When people are afraid, they have physiological reactions. They're likely to experience rapid breathing, become lightheaded and sweaty, and feel muscle tension, all while stress hormones are flooding their body. The fight, flight, or freeze response is an instinctive reaction to stress.

Your body is actively responding to distress and getting ready to run, fight, or stay immobile. Your reaction to fear or stress may be to lash out with anger or violence, avoid all conflict at any cost and run away, or completely shut down. Whatever your normal response to stress is, frequent stress over time damages your health.

In this chapter, I detail building blocks for becoming stronger in the face of distress. Distress tolerance requires practice. There are a variety of approaches for doing it, and even small changes can produce big benefits.

Self-Soothing

When people feel stress or anxiety, they often look outward for help. For example, some people who suffer from distress look for help from family or friends, seeking comfort or reassurance. Help may come from healthcare professionals in the form of medication or psychotherapy. Still others may seek relief in substances such as alcohol, marijuana, or other drugs.

Self-soothing is looking inward for your comfort. Self-soothing techniques are evidence-based tools for regaining emotional regulation and composure in the face of negative feelings. Learning these tools improves resilience and increases your ability to tolerate the expected stressors in life.

REMEMBER

Self-soothing requires a conscious effort to calm your body and your mind.

TECHNICAL STUFF

Many of the skills found throughout this chapter are adaptations from dialectical behavior therapy (DBT), which is a form of cognitive therapy developed by Dr. Marcia Linehan in the 1980s. Linehan's therapy was introduced to help those with severe mental health problems that included suicidal thoughts and attempts. However, over the years, DBT skills have helped those who suffer stress, anxiety, depression, OCD, and other mental health concerns. For more information check out *DBT For Dummies* by Gillian Galen and Blaise Aguirre (Wiley).

Exercising

Regular exercise improves your cardiovascular system, strengthens your bones and muscles. It keeps you younger by preventing muscle loss and decreased bone density caused by aging. And it burns calories and boosts your metabolism, which helps to protect you from obesity and diabetes. Regular exercise also helps you to sleep better, which keeps you energized and helps your body (especially your brain) recover and repair itself. Exercise also improves memory and focus.

Exercise has a particularly significant, very positive impact on mental health. Exercise is a natural mood booster. It releases feel-good endorphins into the body and decreases stress, anxiety, and depression. It leads to increased self-esteem and well-being and adds to resilience.

TIP

For people with OCD, exercise is a particularly good habit because of its ability to reduce the distress associated with obsessions. Studies have shown that regular exercise can decrease the frequency and severity of both obsessions and compulsions.

Relaxing

Taking time out of each day to relax also decreases stress. It can improve digestion, increase blood flow, provide an energy boost, lower blood pressure, and even reduce inflammation. Relaxation also improves emotional well-being. Like other forms of self-soothing, relaxation helps to regulate your stress hormones and emotions, and it leads to improved *resilience* (the ability to weather stressful situations).

People have different ways of relaxing. For you, it could be spending time outside enjoying the sunlight or nature. Or reading something for pleasure. You may prefer drinking a cup of tea and taking a quiet moment to yourself.

Deep breathing

Deep breathing may be one way of relaxing, but it should also be in your toolkit as a way to settle down at any time. Deep breathing promotes immediate relief by slowing heart rate, reducing blood pressure, and reducing the stress hormones in your body. It increases the flow of oxygen throughout the body, signaling the brain to calm down. Other benefits of deep breathing include:

- Improved digestion
- Decreased pain
- Decreased depression
- Decreased anxiety
- Improved respiratory function

There are many forms of deep breathing. Different strokes for different folks. Try out a few and see what works for you.

TIP

Here are a few tips to remember with whatever technique you choose:

- Take a moment to relax your body. Shrug your shoulders, wiggle your neck, relax your face, soften your eyes.
- Either sit up straight or lie down, whichever you prefer.
- Practice at least a few minutes every day.

Here are a few samples of different breathing techniques:

- **Box breathing:** Breathe in through your nose as you count to four, hold for a count of four, breathe out for a count of four, hold for a count of four. Repeat.
- **Belly breathing:** Place one hand on your belly and the other hand on your chest. Inhale deeply through your nose. Make sure that your belly rises higher than your chest. Exhale and repeat.
- **Pursed-lip breathing:** Take a deep breath in, and then exhale very slowly through your mouth with your lips close together, making a soft sound or whistle. Repeat.
- **4-7-8 breathing:** Exhale deeply. Inhale for four seconds, hold for seven seconds, and exhale for eight seconds. Repeat.
- **Cocoon breathing:** Inhale deeply with your eyes open. Hold for a few seconds. Then, as you exhale, slowly close your eyes. Imagine a warm curtain covering you. With each round, go deeper into the cocoon.

- **Tactical breathing:** Inhale deeply for four seconds. Hold. Exhale for four seconds. Repeat.
- **Cyclic breathing:** Inhale deeply once, followed by a shorter inhale, and then exhale very slowly. Repeat.

TECHNICAL STUFF

Recent research at Stanford University found that cyclic breathing is highly effective in reducing anxiety. The study found that during a randomized-controlled study, cyclic breathing decreased anxiety and negative mood and increased positive feelings more than other types of breathing exercises. This effect was produced with just five minutes of cyclic breathing during the one-month experiment. Worth a try!

TIP

For many more breathing exercises and detailed instructions, including guided audio to listen to, check out *Breathing Exercises For Dummies* by Shamash Alidina (Wiley).

Changing temperature

Changing the temperature of your body can be a successful distress tolerance strategy. Some people find that a warm bath or shower calms them down. Others use a cold compress or splash of cold water to decrease an emotional response. Applying ice to the face or wrists can also startle your body and decrease whatever emotional response you may be having.

These strategies are highly personal. Some people find sitting in a warm bath boring or even get more nervous. Others may experience soaking highly relaxing. Add soothing music or candles to enhance the experience.

You can think of applying cold to the face as similar to throwing cold water on someone who is panicked or hysterical. Panic often increases body temperature. But some people find it extremely irritating. Do whatever helps you.

TECHNICAL STUFF

When a mammal falls into extremely cold water, there is an instant physiological reaction. The heart rate and nervous system instantly slow down. This is called the *dive reflex*, and it may be the reason that extremely cold water or ice can calm someone who is highly agitated.

Meditating

Meditation is an extremely useful tool to help improve your ability to handle stressful emotions. It's especially good for those who suffer from OCD because it involves practicing being focused on the here and now.

TIP

People with OCD should not view meditation as a technique to stop obsessions, but as a way to accept thoughts as simply thoughts. By doing that, the thoughts become less demanding.

There are multiple forms of meditation, but most focus on concentrating on one particular thing, such as breathing, walking, looking at a candle, or doing a certain exercise such as yoga or t'ai chi.

WARNING

Some meditation practices involve saying certain mantras, which may be a word, a phrase, or a sound. There is some danger of the specific mantra becoming a compulsive reaction to an obsession, so I don't suggest that you use mantra meditation.

Many studies suggest using meditation as a complementary treatment for OCD. The main benefit of meditation for OCD is a significant reduction in the severity of symptoms. However, studies of the general population suggest that it has many other benefits such as:

- Reducing stress hormones in the body and, therefore, reducing anxiety and panic
- Improving attention span and mental clarity
- Lowering blood pressure
- Improving sleep
- Helping to manage chronic pain
- Reducing negative thoughts

If you choose to start a meditation practice, start with small goals. Even a few minutes can be helpful if you can make yourself do it somewhat regularly. I don't want to add more rules or responsibilities to your life, so think about five minutes a day to begin. Try to find a time in your day that you have five minutes, just before a meal or after making your bed. It doesn't matter when you do it, but scheduling it helps you remember to do it.

TIP

Many meditation apps allow you to choose how long your meditation session takes. Start with five minutes. If that seems endless, cut it back to two or three.

For people with OCD, I suggest guided meditation. These meditations are led by someone either on an app or verbally and provides you with structure. Especially in the beginning, having someone's voice guide you through your practice helps you focus. There are many apps available; some are free and others offer subscriptions. You can almost always get a free trial to try one out.

TIP

Here are a few tips for starting a practice:

- Find a quiet place away from distractions.
- Turn your phone to silent mode.
- Make sure you feel comfortable either sitting or lying down.
- When you feel comfortable, close your eyes.
- Sit quietly and allow thoughts to come and go.
- Do not judge how well you meditate. All is good.

TIP

It's perfectly normal to have thoughts throughout your meditation practice. With consistency, they'll become softer and less frequent.

Engaging in pleasurable activities

When people are stressed — whether because of OCD, depression, or anxiety — they tend to get stuck in patterns of just getting through their days the best that they can. Some people struggle to even complete their daily responsibilities. People often become mired in distress and withdraw from activities. Almost all people with mental health problems put off seeking pleasure.

A key component in developing better stress tolerance is to incorporate pleasurable activities into your daily routines. Not only do these activities introduce a bit of distraction from the daily grind, but they improve mood by increasing positive brain chemicals and decreasing stress hormones. In addition, engaging in pleasurable activities is associated with lower blood pressure and better physical function.

Pleasurable activities should be voluntary and free from the demands of work. Some activities are brief and give you a quick respite such as a quick walk outside. Others, like vacations, regular exercise, or volunteering, may help repair or restore your mind and body from stress. Here are a few examples:

- Attending an interesting class or lecture
- Attending a pleasurable event
- Camping
- Collecting
- Cooking
- Crafting
- Engaging in hobbies
- Exercising
- Gardening
- Getting together with friends
- Having a spa day
- Hiking
- Listening to or playing music
- Making art
- Playing a game
- Playing cards
- Playing tennis
- Reading
- Taking a vacation

- Volunteering
- Walking outside
- Writing

Of course, there are endless examples of pleasurable activities. You may have your own that's not on this list. The important point is to make sure you engage in pleasurable activities regularly. That can be pretty hard to do when you're feeling down and defeated. But moving forward sometime requires doing things you don't really feel like doing at the time.

TIP

Find something mentally engaging enough so that you can briefly forget about your troubles. Make engaging in pleasurable activities part of your journey into better mental health.

Making a distress tolerance plan

A *distress tolerance plan* is a personal plan for handling distress without becoming overwhelmed. Table 13-1 is an example of a plan from Tara who suffers from checking OCD. Her goal is to reduce the amount of time she spends checking her locks from two hours a day to 15 minutes a day. She's working with a therapist to accomplish this goal.

TABLE 13-1 Tara's Distress Tolerance Plan

Activity	Why It May Help	Response to Trying It Out
Breathing	I've used it in the past.	When I was doing box breathing before resisting checking the locks, it helped me calm down.
Exercising	I need to do it because I hate being so out of shape.	My therapist helped me decide to join a group exercise class. I loved the music and had fun. I actually forgot about my OCD for an hour.
Having a spa day	I don't take care of myself.	Actually, it made me nervous just sitting there. I don't think this one will help.
Cooking	I used to like to cook before my OCD got so bad.	I made a simple pasta dish and a salad. My family was so happy, and it made me feel good.
Playing a game	When the kids were little, they loved playing charades with me. I liked it, too.	I felt pretty silly at first. But I played charades with my family. We had popcorn and actually enjoyed ourselves.

In Worksheet 13-1, develop your own distress tolerance plan. Consider what activities you want to try out yourself. In the first column, write your strategy. In the second column write a reason you might find this particularly helpful. In the third column, describe your reaction to using the strategy. You may want to save some blank spaces for later in case one or more technique doesn't work.

WORKSHEET 13-1 My Distress Tolerance Plan

Activity	Why It May Help	Response to Trying It Out

TIP

Don't forget to include at least one or two pleasurable activities.

Some people feel that building distress tolerance improves their outlook and helps them feel more powerful. What are your feelings after completing this exercise? Write about them in Worksheet 13-2.

WORKSHEET 13-2 My Reflections on Distress Tolerance

____

____

____

____

____

____

____

____

____

____

____

____

____

____

____

____

Radical Acceptance: It Is What It Is

Accepting reality can be difficult. When bad things happen, whether to yourself or others, you may have a tendency to question why:

- » Why do I suffer so much?
- » Why do people get sick and die?
- » Why can't I stop washing my hands?
- » Why are people mean to each other?
- » Why is there so much traffic?
- » Why do I have so many weird thoughts?
- » Why am I so anxious all the time?
- » Why was I traumatized?
- » Why did my loved one leave me?

- Why am I so unhappy?
- Why is life so unfair?
- Why do I have chronic pain?
- Why do I have so many obsessions?

Accepting reality as it is, rather than fighting it, means giving up those unanswerable questions. There will inevitably be loss, disappointment, and pain in your lifetime. Radical acceptance tells you to take the cards you're dealt and play them the best you can.

Radical acceptance means acknowledging what's happening even when it's painful, unwanted, or uncomfortable. You don't pretend that everything is okay, but you look at what's happening objectively. You stop the struggle.

If you have OCD or depression or anxiety, you accept those unpleasant feelings. When you can't stand the feelings or believe that they're somehow unfair, you pile more negative feelings on top. Radical acceptance helps people move from feeling that life is unfair to taking stock of their situations in a realistic way. You calmly consider the facts and the possible alternatives. Then you either accept or change the best way you can.

REMEMBER

Instead of staying stuck, acceptance paves the way toward changing what you can change and leaving judgment behind. It increases resilience and allows movement toward living a better life.

Affirmations for radical acceptance

Radical acceptance requires consistent practice of letting go of the struggle to change the unchangeable. It boosts your resilience and ability to handle the obstacles and challenges that living a life involves. Instead of criticizing yourself or your situation, try to accept what's happening but change your thoughts to something more positive. Affirmations are one way to practice acceptance.

Here are some examples that you can use when faced with difficult situations or emotions:

- What has happened in the past is past. I can accept that without judgment.
- I don't like what's happening, but I'm handling it the best I can.
- What is reality is not going to change.
- Sometimes I fail, but sometimes I succeed.
- I can deal with difficult emotions.
- I can only control my reactions.
- I am not perfect, and that is okay.
- I feel pain and don't like it, but it's what I feel.
- I can accept what life gives to me.
- I will change what I can and accept what I can't change.

- I am strong and can handle what comes to me.
- I've gotten through tough times before.
- I have limitations. I am human.
- This is uncomfortable, but I can tolerate it.
- I am at peace with what I have.

Repeating affirmations is different from being overly optimistic. Reality can be full of problems, failures, rejections, and negative emotions. Affirmations can help you accept these difficulties but maintain hope that life can be tolerated, solutions are sometimes possible, and there are always opportunities for growth.

TIP

In Worksheet 13-3, write a few affirmations that speak to you and keep them in a file or list on your phone. Pull them out when you feel stressed or anxious.

WORKSHEET 13-3 My Affirmations

____

____

____

____

____

____

____

____

____

Opposite actions

The opposite actions technique is useful in everyday life, regardless of whether you're stressed, anxious, depressed, or angry. Simply put, when you have a negative emotional response, make yourself do the opposite behavior. By practicing opposite actions, you can retrain your brain from automatically repeating unhealthy patterns. Here are some emotions and how you can perform the opposite action:

- **Anger:** When people get angry, they generally lash out — they yell, swear, hit, push, and are usually obnoxious. When you feel angry, instead of lashing out, try to speak softly, slow your breathing, and say something kind or at least neutral. Relax your facial muscles.
- **Ashamed or guilty:** People who feel guilty usually try to hide. The opposite action is to move forward confidently and apologize if you can. Realize that everyone makes mistakes.

- **Depressed or sad:** The natural tendency for those who are sad is to withdraw from others and become inactive. Instead, make yourself reach out to friends or family. Or go out and exercise. Be active.
- **Anxious or stressed:** People with anxiety avoid situations that could possibly make themselves more anxious. Go out and be with other people. Expose yourself slowly to what makes you anxious (see Part 3 for more on exposure).

TIP

While you're doing the opposite action, relax the muscles in your face and gently smile. Think of the *Mona Lisa* smile — just a subtle change to your face can help you perform the opposite action smoothly and successfully.

What are some of the affirmations that you think may help you with radical acceptance. What are your feelings about radical acceptance? Are there times that you may choose to do the opposite action? How would that help you? Write about this subject in Worksheet 13-4.

WORKSHEET 13-4 My Reflections on Opposite Actions

5 Exploring Additional Treatments

IN THIS PART . . .

Examine the concept of acceptance.

Become more focused on present moments.

Recognize the values most important to you.

Decide to live a life consistent with your values.

Understand the role of medications in the treatment of OCD.

Take an honest look at the costs and benefits of medication.

Examine the evidence of alternative treatments.

IN THIS CHAPTER

» Staying focused on now

» Building some tolerance skills

» Deciding what's important

Chapter 14 Accepting, Committing, and Getting Better

If you have obsessive-compulsive disorder (OCD), you probably experience lots of discomfort, distress, and worry. Hours of your day may be spent obsessing and either actively avoiding things or compulsively responding to your obsessions.

Acceptance and commitment therapy (ACT) is an evidence-based treatment for OCD. Instead of facing fears head on, ACT helps people change their relationship to their beliefs, thoughts, and feelings. The theory behind ACT helps you accept discomfort as part of life instead of struggling or fighting. With acceptance comes the commitment to live a life that is consistent with your own personal values. Life can be difficult, but focusing on making it meaningful decreases distressing symptoms.

This chapter outlines some of the basic premises of ACT and how they apply to OCD. A willingness to experience life and to live life well is the goal of ACT.

TECHNICAL STUFF

ACT is often used in conjunction with exposure and response prevention (ERP), which I cover in Part 3. ACT and DBT (see Chapter 13) are both therapies developed under the umbrella of cognitive behavioral therapy (CBT). There are subtle differences in their focus, but they all integrate the various reciprocal relationships between thinking, feeling, and behaving.

Understanding Acceptance

Acceptance involves an open awareness of the present moment, whether it's pleasant or not. It calls for a willingness to accept reality without judging it. When you feel upset, embrace your feelings rather than fight them. When you struggle to keep discomfort out of your life, you become more upset because life is inevitably full of distress. By stopping the need to avoid all discomfort, you actually make those times less difficult.

Dropping the rope

One of my favorite metaphors often cited by those who practice ACT is referred to as a tug of war with a monster. This metaphor illustrates how fighting against obsessions, worries, or other unwanted feelings is a fruitless battle.

Consider your OCD a monster. The monster is 100 feet tall and weighs 200 tons. You hate having OCD. You're engaged in a battle with it. You hold one side of the rope, and your OCD monster holds the other. The two of you are standing on either side of a great canyon.

When I say, "Go," start pulling. How can you win the battle? Surely your gigantic monster will win. That monster will pull you right into the canyon. You only have one move. Drop the rope. The monster tumbles back and falls on their butt. By letting go of the struggle, you can go on with your day.

In Worksheet 14-1, take a few minutes and write about a situation in which you can drop the rope.

TIP

I use this metaphor frequently with clients. It's especially good when you're engaged in an unwinnable relationship squabble. Dropping the rope lets you step away from a fruitless fight.

Thanking your thoughts

Evolution primes humans to look out for danger. That makes sense — it's a way of protecting you and preparing to handle slips, falls, disasters, or attacks from other people or animals. People with OCD have a malfunctioning danger alarm. It's constantly sounding the alarm and predicting the horrible possibilities of the future.

TIP

A key technique in ACT is to build a skill that puts distance between you and your thoughts. It requires you to step back and objectively look at your distressing thoughts. The concept involves learning that you aren't your thoughts. Instead of thinking you're a loser, you relabel the thought and say, "I'm having a thought that I might be a loser."

TIP

Another way to reduce the power of obsessional thinking is to consider these thoughts just as passing mental events holding little importance. When you have an obsession, thank your mind for that thought. Especially when you're first working with this concept, it's good to say it out loud. It may sound a bit corny, but the technique defuses the emotional impact of an obsession. Table 14-1 provides a few examples.

WORKSHEET 14-1 My Reflections on When I Can Drop the Rope

TABLE 14-1 Examples of Thanking the Mind

Thought	Thank You
I'm sure this countertop is contaminated and I'll get sick if I don't clean it.	Thank you, mind, for that thought. I know you're trying to keep me safe.
I think I might scream out obscenities in synagogue today. I'd better not go.	Great thinking. I know you're worried even though it's never happened.
I might drop the baby in the bath.	Very nice thought, but that doesn't really help me do what I need to do. I'm always careful with the baby.
I'm sure I'll make a mistake, and I have to check again and again.	Thank you, mind, but if I keep checking, I'll never get this done.
I can't stop straightening the fringe on the rug. If I don't keep it straight, bad things will happen.	I know you mean well, mind, but if I listen to you, I won't get to work on time.

When you have an obsession — whether it's a thought, an impulse, or an image — take the time to thank your mind and return to what you were doing. Don't expect immediate results — it takes some practice. The goal is to decrease the power of an obsession and increase the flexibility of your thinking. Try this exercise out in Worksheet 14-2.

WORKSHEET 14-2 Thanking Your Mind

Thought	Thank You

TIP

Another way to defuse the power of a thought is to sing it out loud or say it in a silly voice. *Remember:* It's just a thought, not necessarily reality.

Practicing mindfulness

Mindfulness involves getting in touch with what's actually happening in the here and now. When you consider what upsets you, it's usually worries about the future such as:

- Will I get sick from not cleaning sufficiently?
- If I don't check the locks on the windows, will someone come and kill my family?
- What if I soil my pants when I go to the store?
- What if I run over someone with my car and hurt them?

Or you feel regret and guilt about what happened in the past. Here are some examples:

- What if I didn't get all the disgusting dirt off my hands?
- What if I made a mistake and I get fired?
- Did I say something horrible that made my partner mad?
- My partner left me because I screwed up the relationship.

When you spend your time in the past or future, you may very likely ruin your present moment. Even when your present moment is difficult, it's probably better than what your mind imagines.

Take a few minutes to feel what's going on right now. Observe your feelings and thoughts objectively, as if you were a scientist. Take a step back from your thoughts and feelings. Thoughts are only brief mental events passing through your life. They don't always represent accurate representations of reality. Feelings are fleeting. View the present dispassionately and without judgment. Work through all these thoughts in Worksheet 14-3.

WORKSHEET 14-3 Accepting the Present Moment

Questions	Answers
Take mental stock of your body. Do you have pain? Are you breathing fast or slow? Describe what you feel objectively. Don't judge.	
Continue monitoring your body. Are there changes? Do sensations build or lessen? Predict how long they'll last.	
Notice the thoughts that are going through your mind. Imagine that the thoughts are leaves floating down a stream. Put each thought on a leaf and watch it disappear.	
Predict how long these thoughts will occur. Will they continue all day or longer? Watch them float away. Predict how important these thoughts will be in a month or a year.	
What are you feeling? Anxious, sad, worried? How strong are those feelings? Sit with them. Observe them. Don't struggle. Write what you feel.	
Have your feelings changed? Increased or decreased? Accept them now. They will change overtime. Write about your experience here.	

In Worksheet 14-4, take a moment to reflect on staying in the present moment. Do you think actively and nonjudgmentally staying focused in the here and now will help your OCD? If so, how?

WORKSHEET 14-4 My Reflections on Staying in the Present Moment

Getting in Touch with Your Values

When you're stuck in an endless loop of obsessions and compulsions, your life is full of distress and worry. Is that how you want to live your life? Probably not. When you're fully caught up in your OCD world, you have little time to pursue other activities.

In this section, you focus on living a life consistent with your larger values. *Values* are the core principles that matter to you, such as being connected with your family, being kind to others, or doing purposeful work.

REMEMBER

ACT involves accepting life as it is and living a life that is meaningful and aligned with your personal values.

Clarifying your values

Everyone has a different set of values. You may not spend much time thinking about your values, but they act as a compass that guides your behavior across many situations. Values influence your attitudes, your interactions with others, and your actions.

Your values help you make decisions in your personal life and your professional life. They act as a filter through which you evaluate your world and motivate you to act in ways that are consistent with those deeply held beliefs. Values may develop during childhood, through spiritual pursuits, culture, education, or self-reflection.

In Worksheet 14-5, you'll find a list of common values is presented. The list certainly can't capture every possible value, but it includes the most common ones. Circle your top ten values or add your own at the end of the worksheet.

WORKSHEET 14-5 Clarifying Your Values

Acceptance	Accomplishment	Adventure
Authenticity	Balance	Belonging
Beauty	Cleanliness and neatness	Comfort
Control	Creativity	Compassion
Courage	Curiosity	Decisiveness
Dependability	Devotion	Dignity
Education/Learning	Empathy	Fairness and honesty
Family and friends	Fun	Giving to others
Gratitude	Health	Humility
Independence	Love	Making a difference
Motivation	Being open to experiences	Patience
Passion	Predictability	Self-awareness
Supportiveness	Tradition	Tranquility
Variety	Wealth	Winning
Wisdom	Youthfulness	Zeal

Identifying your core values

Your core values are a guide that helps you decide what you do day to day. However, many people are so caught up with their struggles that they don't think about what living a life guided by values would even look like. Clarifying your own top values helps you become more aware of the life you'd like to live.

After completing the values clarification quiz, write down the top ten in column one of Worksheet 14-6. Then, in the second column, write a phrase or sentence about what that value means to you.

WORKSHEET 14-6 My Top Ten Values

Value	What It Means to Me
1.	
2.	
3.	
4.	
5.	
6.	
7.	
8.	
9.	
10.	

Living a value-driven life

Consider your top-ten values from Worksheet 14-6. Of those, which are the most important to you? In Worksheet 14-7, write your top three values in the first column. In the second column, write about how you're planning to accomplish or live in support of those values.

WORKSHEET 14-7 My Top Three Values

Value	How I Accomplish This Value
1.	
2.	
3.	

After you've thought about living a value-driven life, are you ready to make some changes? Why or why not? Reflect on that in Worksheet 14-8.

WORKSHEET 14-8 My Reflections on Whether I'm Ready to Live a Value-Driven Life

IN THIS CHAPTER

» Taking a look at medications for OCD

» Deciding whether to try medication

» Digging deep into brain stimulation

Chapter 15 Biological Treatments

The first-line treatment for obsessive-compulsive disorder (OCD) is exposure and response prevention (ERP), which is a type of cognitive behavioral therapy (CBT). ERP involves gradually facing obsessional fear in a slow, structured way.

Some people with OCD aren't good candidates for ERP therapy — perhaps because they can't access the right treatment, their symptoms don't respond to therapy, they feel uncomfortable going to a therapist, they can't afford psychotherapy, they lack insight into their obsessions, or their symptoms are extremely severe. If ERP is not appropriate for you, medications may help.

Many people also take medication while being treated with ERP. That's because the medication sometimes decreases distress enough so the person can tolerate ERP.

In this chapter, I review the pros and cons of medication, detail which medications are supported by evidence to work, and give you some information about brain stimulation.

Making the Medication Decision

Taking medication for a mental health disorder is a decision that should be made by the client in collaboration with their mental health provider. Full remission is quite uncommon with medication only, and the positive response ranges from about 40 percent to 65 percent. (In contrast, between 65 percent and 80 percent of people respond positively to ERP, a specialized form of psychotherapy.) Between 25 percent and 40 percent of people with OCD do not respond at all to medication. Therefore, decisions about medication should be carefully considered.

Prior to making any decision, you should have a complete physical examination to assess your current physical health. Be sure to inform your provider about any other health problems you have. In addition, tell your provider if you have:

- Insomnia (either trouble going to sleep or trouble staying asleep)
- Periods of time where you don't sleep for days
- Substance use or abuse
- Poor appetite
- Fatigue
- Any herbal supplements you take
- Your history of (or current) anxiety or depression
- Thoughts about suicide or previous suicide attempts

Psychotropic medication affects the functioning of the brain and changes mood, alertness, and perception. These medications are typically used to treat a wide range of mental health problems, such as depression, anxiety, attention deficit disorders, and schizophrenia, as well as OCD.

TIP

Although primary care providers prescribe the vast majority of psychotropic medications, the treatment of OCD requires knowledge of the doses and types of drugs prescribed. If you're seeing a primary care provider, ask whether they have experience and knowledge of treating OCD.

Approved medications for OCD

Medications that are used to treat OCD are most often those that increase certain *neurotransmitters* (chemical messengers) in your brain. The primary medications used are usually selective serotonin reuptake inhibitors (SSRIs), which are also commonly prescribed for anxiety or depression. These medications increase the amount of serotonin in the brain.

REMEMBER

Disruptions in communication between brain neurons are thought to lead to a feeling of being stuck on thoughts and compelled to do certain actions. See Chapter 4 for more information about the causes of OCD.

The U.S. Food and Drug Administration (FDA) has approved the following medications for the treatment of OCD:

- Fluoxetine (Prozac)
- Fluvoxamine (Luvox)
- Paroxetine (Paxil), only for adults
- Sertraline (Zoloft)
- Clomipramine (rarely used because of its side effects)

Higher-than-usual doses are often required to treat OCD. Frequently more than one medication may be tried to find the best match. Treatment generally takes longer to be effective than with depression or anxiety disorders.

WARNING

Another class of drugs, benzodiazepines, also reduces anxiety or stress. They're commonly known as mild tranquilizers. They include Xanax (alprazolam), Valium (diazepam), and Ativan (lorazepam). All these drugs depress the central nervous system and are very effective in reducing anxiety. However, benzodiazepines are also addictive and can lead to other serious health issues. These drugs are not recommended in the treatment of OCD because of their addiction potential. In addition, the depressed nervous system interferes with the learning process during ERP. In order to benefit from ERP, there must be some anxiety or distress.

TECHNICAL STUFF

Other medications, such as citalopram and escitalopram are also used off-label as determined by the prescribing provider. Using a drug *off-label* is the practice of using a medication that is approved by the FDA, but not for that particular reason. For example, someone who does not respond to the first prescribed medication may do better on another, similar medication that doesn't have the official approval of the FDA. In severe cases of OCD, prescribers sometimes add other drugs to help control symptoms. These drugs are usually antipsychotic ones. Side effects of antipsychotic drugs include an increased risk of diabetes, weight gain, and uncontrollable movements called *tardive dyskinesia.*

Positive aspects of medication

Research shows that people with OCD respond better to medication than they do to a *placebo* (an inactive, sham drug such as a sugar pill that people expect may help). Those who respond to medication usually report between 20 percent and 40 percent reduction in symptom severity. Although that sounds pretty low, it may make a huge difference in the lives of OCD sufferers. Those who do respond may be able to return to productive and meaningful lives.

Unfortunately, almost half of people on medication do not respond at all. In addition, full remission is very uncommon, with only about 10 percent reporting no symptoms at all. Medication is typically prescribed for about one or two years after the symptoms improve. Then a gradual tapering of the dosage is done. Unfortunately, when medication is stopped, many people relapse.

REMEMBER

Most professionals agree that ERP is the preferred method of helping those with OCD. Even when taking medication, for most people, psychotherapy should also be part of the treatment plan.

TIP

Here are some situations in which medication may be an appropriate choice:

- **If your thinking is irrational or confused:** If you have trouble concentrating or your thoughts are frequently out of control, medication may help. After the medication takes effect, I still encourage you to seek psychotherapy.
- **If you're having suicidal thoughts or you have plans of suicide:** If that's the case, you should have an immediate evaluation. Call the Suicide and Crisis Lifeline at 988, call 911, or go to the nearest emergency room if you feel in danger of harming yourself. Help is available 24/7.
- **If you have other major mental health issues, such as panic disorder or depression:** When OCD is complicated with another disorder, medication is sometimes necessary for treatment to proceed.

* **If you have bipolar disorder:** Bipolar disorder consists of significant mood swings. People with bipolar disorder generally need help stabilizing moods with medication.
* **If your OCD is very severe:** If your OCD is so severe that you aren't able to work or take care of your daily responsibilities, medication may help decrease the severity of your symptoms enough so you can function and hopefully start psychotherapy.
* **If you won't try ERP because of fear or if you've tried therapy and decided it doesn't work:** Medication may take the edge off of your fear or resistance enough so you can engage in therapy.
* **If you don't have the resources for psychotherapy:** Your insurance may not pay for the sessions needed for treatment or you may not have the time. Or perhaps you live in an area that doesn't have trained mental health professionals. In these circumstances, medication may be a good option. However, for lasting results, therapy is still recommended. With medication and supplemental self-help, you may be able to achieve a significant reduction in suffering.

Side effects of medication

Psychotropic medications help many people with OCD and other mental health disorders. However, there are often significant side effects. Some people experience only very brief, mild side effects that go away with time. Generally, even uncomfortable side effects decrease after a week or two.

TIP

If you're pregnant, may become pregnant, or breastfeeding, talk to your doctor or your child's pediatrician about safe medications to use during those times. Consider psychotherapy as a safe alternative.

Side effects of SSRIs, the most common treatment used for OCD, include the following:

* Constipation
* Diarrhea
* Dizziness
* Dry mouth
* Headaches
* Nausea
* Tremors
* Weight gain

If you suffer any of these side effects, discuss them with your provider. Sometimes the passage of time or other medications can decrease any uncomfortable side effects. Don't stop taking any medication without talking first with your prescriber.

Sexual problems — including loss of sexual drive and problems achieving orgasm — are also common with the use of antidepressants. These side effects can often be treated with an additional medication and usually go away with time.

Suicide risk is also a concern. That's especially common with children, teens, and young adults. Usually, any suicidal thoughts or intentions happen in the beginning weeks of treatment. All people on antidepressants should be monitored by their prescriber in the first few months of treatment. Any suicidal thoughts should be taken seriously.

WARNING

If, after starting an antidepressant, you become agitated and irritable, hopeless, unable to sleep, or aggressive, or if you have unusual behaviors, worsening depression, thoughts about dying, suicidal thoughts, or thoughts of harming yourself, call your healthcare provider. If the threat is imminent, call the Suicide Crisis Lifeline at 988, call 911, or go to an emergency room for treatment.

When you stop taking antidepressants for OCD, you should consult with your doctor so you can avoid or decrease symptoms of *discontinuation syndrome,* which is caused by the chemical changes in your body when you stop taking the medication. Symptoms such as anxiety, stomach upset, or feeling spacey, fatigued, or even as if you have the flu can occur. Discontinuation syndrome can usually be avoided by slowly tapering off your medication. Your prescriber can help you determine how to do that.

Finally, relapse is a consideration to keep in mind when you consider whether to take medication for OCD. Generally, if medication is the only treatment, relapse will likely occur when you stop. Psychotherapy is the preferred treatment for OCD because it decreases the risk of relapse.

WARNING

Clomipramine is an antidepressant that is effective but rarely prescribed unless other medications have been tried and failed. This medication has the same side effects as do the SSRIs, but it also increases the risk of cardiac events and seizures. Careful monitoring is required.

Medication with ERP

Because medication can sometimes help reduce the severity of symptoms, it may be a way to gently introduce the necessary stress of ERP. This approach may have advantages for those whose OCD is moderate to severe.

Medication should be guided by a prescriber who understands the process of ERP. Therapy can help overcome the symptoms and change the way the brain processes information. As successful ERP continues, the dosage can be slowly decreased. When those with OCD are able to manage their symptoms, medication can usually be tapered off.

TIP

Professionals who prescribe antidepressants rarely do psychotherapy, especially ERP. When combining medication with ERP, be sure that the prescriber and the psychotherapist are collaborating.

How to optimize medications

Taking medication is a big deal. Your provider should be willing to take the time to answer any of your questions or concerns. Frequently, people feel rushed during an appointment, or they forget the questions that they wanted to ask. You also may not remember everything the provider said after the appointment. Feel free to take a copy of Worksheet 15-1 with you to your appointment. If you decide to try medication, ask your provider the questions in Worksheet 15-1.

WORKSHEET 15-1 **Questions for My Prescriber**

Question	Answer
Which medication do you recommend? What is the dose?	
Is this medication and dose recommended for treating OCD?	
Are there any foods, drinks, supplements, or other prescriptions I should avoid?	
How long does it typically take for people to see improvement?	
If I don't see improvement after a month or so, will you increase the dose or try something new?	
How often will I check in with you regarding this treatment?	
Are there any side effects that I should be aware of? If I have side effects, how will you manage them?	
How much improvement should I expect?	
How long should I take this medication?	
If the medication doesn't appear to be working, what do you suggest? Are there other options?	
Should I combine taking medication with psychotherapy?	

What are your conclusions about taking medication for your OCD? Reflect on them in Worksheet 15-2.

WORKSHEET 15-2 **My Reflections on Taking Medication**

Considering Brain Stimulation

Brain stimulation is the use of electrical or magnetic impulses to impact specific areas of the brain. It should only be considered when you meet the following criteria:

- » You've made multiple attempts at psychotherapy with a therapist trained in ERP and you haven't responded.
- » You've worked with a medical prescriber and tried various medications without symptom relief.
- » Your OCD is severe and makes it impossible for you to function.
- » You're able to reason and give informed consent, which means that you understand the potential risks and benefits of brain stimulation.

You'll be excluded from treatment if you have other brain disorders such as a traumatic head injury or if you have even a mild stage of dementia. You'll also be excluded if you've been suicidal or had other severe mental health disorders.

TECHNICAL STUFF

Treatment-resistant OCD occurs when people don't get better with multiple attempts of standard evidence-based treatments. Generally, those with OCD who are treatment resistant may be offered brain stimulation.

Noninvasive brain stimulation

Noninvasive brain stimulation is a nonsurgical treatment that uses magnetic fields, ultrasound, or electrical currents applied to the outside of the skull, usually on the scalp, that change the way the brain functions. It can be used to treat different neurological disorders and mental health disorders. The huge advantage of noninvasive strategies is that they're temporary treatments that can be stopped immediately if there are side effects.

Several noninvasive techniques are used for OCD that differ in the way the currents are applied and how deep they go. Here are the most common ones:

- » **Repetitive transcranial magnetic stimulation (rTMS):** Sends electromagnetic pulses to the brain, changing the way neurons respond and communicate in the brain
- » **Deep transcranial magnetic stimulation (dTMS):** Sends magnetic signals deep into the brain, also changing the neuronal activity in the brain
- » **Transcranial direct current stimulation (tDCS):** Uses scalp electrodes to deliver weak electrical currents to the brain, changing the way neurotransmitters work in the brain

All these techniques are safe with few side effects. Some people report mild headaches, others have sensitive spots on their scalps, and some have a transient tingling sensation.

Research has supported the success of treatment with noninvasive brain stimulation for OCD. However, like medication, the results vary widely from person to person.

WARNING

This treatment is not an option for people with metal in their heads, such as shrapnel, bullets, or metal plates. It also isn't safe for people with a history of seizures, brain trauma, or dementia, or those with implanted electronic devices such as pacemakers or nerve stimulators. Children and pregnant or nursing mothers are also excluded.

TECHNICAL STUFF

Some research supports the use of these devices earlier in treatment than usually recommended. Participants who haven't had treatment-refractory OCD often had better results than those with treatment-resistant OCD.

Deep brain stimulation

Deep brain stimulation involves implanting electrodes into certain areas of the brain. Although it is rarely used, it can be quite effective. About 50 percent to 60 percent of patients report a significant reduction in symptoms.

Sort of like a pacemaker of the brain, these electrodes correct faulty circuitry that is involved in the OCD brain. And like a pacemaker, adjustments can be made electronically, and the device can be turned off or removed.

Deep brain stimulation involves a surgery that has risks, such as brain bleeding, infection, or unexpected symptoms resulting from electrical stimulation. Thus, it is reserved for people with severe, chronic, treatment-resistant OCD.

TECHNICAL STUFF

A last-resort treatment for extremely severe cases of OCD in which multiple trials of psychotherapy, medication, and brain stimulation have been attempted without positive result is *ablation*, which targets specific areas of the brain that are related to OCD symptoms. In ablation, special energy sources are used to destroy tiny parts of the brain. The reason this is very rarely used is because it is irreversible, can cause unexpected results, and requires hospitalization. However, some people have made remarkable recoveries after going through the treatment.

What are your thoughts about the possibility of using a brain stimulation treatment for your own OCD? Reflect on this possibility in Worksheet 15-3.

The future of brain stimulation

Brain stimulation procedures may be the future of a large percentage of treatment options for people with OCD and other mental health disorders. Because all thoughts, feelings, and behaviors originate in the brain, targeted treatment will be possible.

WORKSHEET 15-3 My Reflections on Deep Brain Stimulation

Improvements to brain stimulation techniques are being introduced every year. These treatments will become more precise and personalized to the individual patient. Devices will be able to map the actual changes and activities in the brain, and they'll be designed to determine which signals indicate obsessions and compulsions. These maps will be developed during the procedure, making targeting extremely precise.

Artificial intelligence (AI) will be able to collect and analyze huge sets of data to further develop individualized treatment protocols. Advancements in technology will make the treatment cheaper, quicker, and even possibly portable so that patients can access it at home.

The future will likely bring about great improvements in treatment and decrease the suffering of those with OCD.

6 Looking at Sample Treatment Plans

IN THIS PART . . .

Look at different treatment plans for obsessive-compulsive disorder (OCD).

Check out contamination OCD treatment.

Set up a plan to deal with uncertainty and checking OCD.

Recognize the value of being untidy when symmetry is your issue.

Defending against OCD shame and embarrassment.

IN THIS CHAPTER

» Seeing the OCD cycle at work

» Dusting through distortions

» Accepting angst and living life

Chapter 16 Combatting Contamination

Fear of contamination is the most common cause of obsessions and compulsions. This type of obsessive-compulsive disorder (OCD) isn't just a worry about staying clean or keeping things sanitized. Contamination OCD spreads to worry about dirt, body fluids, feces, germs, toxins, chemicals, or any number of imagined sources of possible harm.

People with contamination OCD spend endless hours protecting themselves and others from a myriad of possible dangers. They may endlessly decontaminate and often become prisoners in their own homes for fear of being in situations that they can't control.

This chapter outlines a treatment plan for this common type of OCD. The plan includes exposure and response prevention (ERP), cognitive therapy, distress tolerance, and living a value-driven life. You can revise or follow this plan to fit your own specific triggers, worries, and compulsive actions.

Common Contamination Obsessions and Compulsions

Contamination fears range from getting germs from public toilets, to touching something gross, to other more unusual fears. For example, some people worry about getting contaminated just by being in the same room or even building with someone who may be able to contaminate them. (Chapter 2 offers more examples of contamination fears.)

As I describe in Part 3 of this book, ERP is the most effective treatment for OCD. In this section, you design your own exposure plan.

TIP

Although you can do this exercise on your own, I recommend working with a licensed therapist.

Understanding the worry cycle for contamination OCD

The OCD worry cycle starts with an obsession — a thought, image, or impulse. Next, there is a sense of discomfort, anxiety, or distress, followed by either a deliberate avoidance of the distressful situation or a compulsive act that brings temporary relief.

Table 16-1 shows an example of a Joshua's contamination OCD worry cycle for contamination OCD. He has a strong aversion to anything that may be related to death, believing that somehow he could become ill or even die if he sees, touches, or is near the feared person or object. His OCD has spread over time to dictate what he can accomplish every day.

TABLE 16-1 Joshua's OCD Worry Cycle for Contamination OCD

Question	Answer
What are the specific situations or places that trigger my obsessions?	Seeing a black object — it could be a car, someone's clothes, a cat, or anything that's black or very dark. Also, I can't talk to someone who has lost a close family member. I won't drive near a funeral home or cemetery. If I think about death or dying, I have to take off my clothes and wash them, and then take a long, hot shower. I think about death and dying all the time.
What do I think will happen if I get contaminated?	I might get very sick and possibly die.
How much distress do I feel? A little? A lot? A great deal?	I'm on edge all the time. It's hard for me to work or be out anywhere. I have some part-time data-entry work that I can do at home, but when I get really bad, I can barely do that. I feel horrible and scared.
What do I do to help myself with the distress? What do I avoid? What actions do I perform to protect myself and others?	Mostly I avoid going out. When I have to go out, I'm very nervous and carry a bible with me. I have some favorite scripture passages that I've underlined and repeat when I think I've been exposed. I usually shower and wash my clothes when I get back. I recite bible verses constantly, hoping for some protection.
How much relief do I feel after avoiding or acting? For how long?	It helps for a few minutes, sometimes up to an hour or so, but all my fears come back pretty quickly. I feel like I'm living in hell.

As you can tell, Joshua's OCD causes him to live an isolated and lonely life. He can barely work enough to take care of his bills and spends hours showering, avoiding, and chanting passages from the bible. He feels afraid during most of his waking hours.

In Worksheet 16-1, describe your own OCD worry cycle. If you're working with a therapist, you can either work with them to fill it out or bring in the filled-out worksheet for feedback. You may also consider sharing your responses with a trusted family member or friend who knows you very well.

WORKSHEET 16-1 My OCD Worry Cycle

Question	Answer
What are the specific situations or places that trigger my obsessions?	
What do I think will happen if I get contaminated?	
How much distress do I feel? A little? A lot? A great deal?	
What do I do to help myself with the distress? What do I avoid? What actions do I perform to protect myself and others?	
How much relief do I feel after avoiding or acting? For how long?	

After completing the exercise, you may have some strong feelings. Some people feel relief that they understand their own issues. Others feel overwhelmed and frightened about how they can possibly get better. Don't worry, there's more work to be done. You can get through this.

In Worksheet 16-2, reflect on the thoughts and feelings you have after describing your OCD cycle. Do you feel more confident that you understand your own pattern?

WORKSHEET 16-2 My Reflections on My OCD Worry Cycle

Preparing a list and rating the ugh factor

Now that you've described your OCD cycle, it's time to make a list. On this list, you'll describe all your OCD triggers and how much stress they cause you. But first, take a look at Joshua's list about the triggers that cause him distress about death and dying (see Table 16-2).

REMEMBER

The ugh factor is a scale from 0 to 10, where 0 means no distress at all, 5 is moderate distress, and 10 means jumping out of your skin.

TABLE 16-2 Joshua's Trigger List and Ugh Factor Rating

Trigger	Ugh Factor (0–10)
Seeing a black cat	7
Hearing about someone I know getting sick	9
Going out anywhere in public	8
Seeing an ambulance or a funeral procession	10+
Being near someone who's wearing black or even noticing black objects around me	5
Thinking about death	9

Now, in Worksheet 16-3, make your own trigger list and rate the ugh factor for your contamination obsessions.

WORKSHEET 16-3 My Trigger List and Ugh Factor Rating

Trigger	Ugh Factor (0–10)

Catching compulsions

Compulsive actions follow obsessions. Here are the most common compulsions related to contamination fears:

- **Excessive washing, bathing, or sanitizing the body:** Frequently people who engage in these compulsions have red, irritated skin. Many have open, bloody sores due to repeated washing. They may use special cleaners, disinfectants, or soaps and engage in special washing rituals.
- **Cleaning or sanitizing articles or spaces excessively:** Special supplies, ordering, and counting are usually part of the compulsion. Their procedures have to be "just right," or they may need to repeat them. Washing clothing when returning from any outing is common.

- **Avoiding certain possibly contaminated places or wearing protective clothing:** Some people with contamination OCD rarely leave their home because of fear of becoming contaminated by someone or something outside. They may wear masks when walking around the block. Some have special sprays that they frequently use when it's necessary to leave the house. Many people with contamination OCD arbitrarily determine that some places are clean and others are inherently dirty. This determination isn't based on reason or facts.
- **Discarding or destroying contaminated objects:** Some people may toss into the trash items that are deemed "dirty." Other people may engage in extensive rituals, including burying or burning items they believe to be contaminated.

TIP

Many compulsions are carried out in a certain ritualistic way. For example, someone who washes must wash every finger in a certain order. Those who use avoidance may have special ways of shopping for food that include determining whether something is dirty and needs to be picked up with latex gloves. Other compulsions may include counting or ordering in special ways that make sense only to the person doing them.

What compulsions do you engage in following an obsession about contamination? Are there rituals involved? Jot them down in Worksheet 16-4.

WORKSHEET 16-4 My Reflections on My Compulsions

Starting exposure and response prevention

Now you have the information you need to start your own ERP. You know your triggers, their ugh factor, and your compulsive actions.

TIP

In Chapters 9 and 10, you can find specific directions to begin ERP. You begin by deciding which obsession you work on; then you expose yourself to that trigger; and finally, you resist your compulsion. You fight compulsions by either delaying them or changing them. If avoidance is your compulsion, you slowly begin to expose yourself to the situation or place you avoid.

REMEMBER

Start with something that you're able to do. In other words, go low and slow. Repeat exposures until your distress comes down. Then repeat again.

To help you along with your specific plan, let's return to Joshua who had obsessions about death and dying. Joshua reports some very strong negative feelings about his OCD triggers. If he were in therapy, I would likely attempt to find a few more things that bother him but not quite as much. That's one reason it's a good idea to work with a mental health professional — they can steer you in this direction.

With Joshua, I would start on his least distressing obsession, his fear of someone wearing black or anything that he sees that is black (such as a black cat or car). His compulsion is to avoid black as much as possible.

When he agreed to try exposure, I might bring a black throw blanket to a session and have him look at it for a few minutes. We'd probably engage in some conversation about how upset he is to just look at the blanket. I'd have him rate his ugh factor. After a few minutes, his ugh factor is most likely going to decrease.

Maybe that first session would only include looking at the blanket. But over time, I would gradually increase that exposure to having Joshua touch it, then putting it on his knees, and finally being able to tolerate wearing black by draping it across his shoulders. I would encourage him to wear black to subsequent sessions, and I would wear black, too.

I also might devise some fun activities involving black, such as searching for black objects in the environment, cutting shapes out of black paper, or putting the black blanket on his head. The idea behind going beyond the initial fear is to help Joshua generalize the lesson of exposure to other parts of his life. Almost always, laughter is involved as exposure progresses.

These exposures would almost certainly take more than one session; it would depend on his tolerance and willingness to handle distress. Usually, after multiple exposures, the color black would become meaningless.

REMEMBER

Psychotherapy is a collaborative process. If at any time the client feels overwhelmed, I back off and do something easier until they can tolerate more difficult exposures.

Have you been able to practice exposure and response prevention? If so, how were your experiences. Think about what you have learned and jot it down in Worksheet 16-5.

WORKSHEET 16-5 My Reflections on ERP

____

____

____

____

____

____

____

____

____

____

____

____

____

____

____

____

____

Dealing with Risks and Uncertainty

Your logical brain knows that there is no such thing as certainty. However, OCD tells you that everything is dangerous and that the risks of not performing your compulsive actions are extreme.

Interestingly, people with OCD don't learn that most uncertain situations are actually safe. They probably won't get sick by touching a can at the grocery store. Their hands aren't really contaminated after making a meal. ERP helps people learn through repeated experiences that most of what is making them fearful is their OCD.

The intolerance of uncertainty is at the heart of many types of OCD, especially contamination fears. Because germs, irritants, poisons, toxins, or other impurities are usually invisible, it's hard to rule out the possibility that they may exist. That's why frequent exposures with response prevention teach people with contamination OCD that their world is relatively safe.

Overestimation of risk is also an integral problem for those with contamination OCD. They may believe that touching a doorknob will certainly make them sick. Or that neglecting or shortening a ten-minute handwash will lead to disease. Again, repetition of ERP can increase awareness of actual risk.

Is fear of uncertainty and overestimating risk part of your OCD beliefs? Write about them in Worksheet 16-6.

WORKSHEET 16-6 My Reflections on Fear of Uncertainty and Overestimating Risk

Defining and Correcting Contaminated Thoughts

Cognitive distortions are exaggerations or misinterpretations of reality (see Chapter 12). They tend to be habitual and irrational. Cognitive distortions often distort reality in a negative way. Here are some common distortions among those with contamination OCD:

- **Catastrophizing:** Believing that even a small exposure to a poison, germ, or other irritant will certainly lead to severe illness

- **Emotional reasoning:** Feeling anxious or afraid of something and then concluding that there must be something to be afraid of
- **Black-and-white reasoning:** Thinking that everything is either entirely clean or filthy, that nothing is just a bit dusty or slightly dirty
- **Dismissing evidence:** Believing that it's just a matter of time before they'll get sick, despite times in the past when they haven't gotten sick from touching contaminated things or being exposed
- **Unreliable forecasting:** Predicting disaster in the future if they don't perform their compulsive cleaning or other rituals

What thought distortions do you find yourself using? Have you been able to work through and see how they influence your feelings and behaviors? Try to come up with some more balanced, reasonable thoughts and jot them down in Worksheet 16-7.

WORKSHEET 16-7 My Reflections on My Thought Distortions

Trying Stress Busters

While working on your contamination OCD, try to incorporate some techniques that enable you to tolerate distress. (Chapter 13 offers complete descriptions.) Here are few ideas:

- Deep breathing
- Exercising or working out
- Splashing cold water on your face
- Holding ice on your wrists
- Accepting discomfort and knowing it will decrease over time
- Delaying compulsive actions for a brief period of time

WARNING

One self-soothing activity that most people with contamination OCD should avoid is soaking in a warm bath or hot tub. That only reinforces the obsession about cleanliness.

Plan some activities that help you to calm down and be self-compassionate. Write out your plan in Worksheet 16-8.

WORKSHEET 16-8 My Plan to Calm Down and Show Myself Compassion

Accepting and Moving Forward

Your contamination OCD makes you uncomfortable, maybe very much so. You're working on getting better, but the results won't be immediate. Although life has been distressing, you've made it. You can tolerate distress.

Now, decide how you want to go on living. Review your values (see Chapter 12) and make a commitment to living a value-driven life. Perhaps you want to devote yourself to your faith, your family, or make the world a better place. Or you may dream of becoming financially successful or just be able to pay your bills on time. You may have always wanted to learn French or study astronomy.

REMEMBER

Whatever you value, it probably isn't to become a prisoner of OCD. Work hard, get better, and live well.

IN THIS CHAPTER

» Checking out checking

» Seeing a circular pattern

» Dealing with doubting

Chapter 17
Curbing Checking

Those with doubting obsessions and checking compulsions live in a constant state of worry and uncertainty. They're driven by the obsessive feeling that something bad may happen to themselves or others. They feel compelled to repetitively and excessively check that these bad things haven't occurred or that they've made adequate attempts to prevent them. This type of OCD consists of a wide variety of doubting obsessions and checking compulsions and is the second most common form of obsessive-compulsive disorder (OCD).

REMEMBER

People with OCD live in a huge tent. Symptoms may overlap and change over time. Someone with checking OCD can also have contamination OCD. Everyone with OCD is unique.

In this chapter, I outline a treatment plan for someone who worries about the possibility of harm due to their neglect or their irresponsibility and engages in compulsive checking behaviors. This plan includes exposure and response prevention (ERP), cognitive therapy, distress tolerance, and acceptance and commitment therapy.

TIP

Be sure to revise this plan to fit your own symptoms. This framework can be especially beneficial if you're working with a therapist.

Doubting and Checking

This type of OCD disrupts everyday life, work, and relationships. The person may be late for appointments, work, or school because of the need to repeatedly check. They become quite irritating to be around because they're often demanding others for reassurance. They ask, "Are you sure I locked the door," or "Do you think I may have insulted our friend?"

Those with checking OCD become confused and lack confidence in their mental ability because of their distrust of their own memory. For example, "I think I turned off the water, but I'm not really sure," or "What if I lost my passport? I think I put it in the safe-deposit box, but I can't remember."

Although the list is infinite, there tend to be certain common themes or fears that result in checking rituals:

- Safety or damage in the home
- Safety to people in the family
- Hit-and-runs (hurting others with your car)
- Injury to others due to negligence
- Inability to make decisions
- Losing important items
- Making mistakes
- Mental reviewing to check for possible harm

The best treatment for OCD is ERP. The following sections help you to develop your own ERP plan.

Understanding the worry cycle for checking OCD

For those with checking OCD, the cycle begins with a feeling of unease. Most often, the obsession is something like, "Did I do something wrong?" or "Did I forget to do make sure everything is okay?"

Next come the checking behaviors, which momentarily offer a sense of relief. However, the relief is brief and the cycle begins again.

Table 17-1 is an example of the worry cycle of someone with checking OCD. Ivy doubts that she's keeping her home secure. She's positive that someone will break in, either when the family is asleep or when they leave the house. Ivy has a routine that she must repeat over and over again to maintain vigilance.

It sounds like Ivy has a pretty stressed-out life. No wonder she's on edge most of the time. Not only does Ivy worry about the safety of her home, but she's also chronically late to work and having trouble getting her work done. Ivy's relationships with her family members and coworkers are strained because of her OCD.

Try to describe your own worry cycle in Worksheet 17-1. You can try this on your own or with your therapist. If you're not in therapy, a very trusted family member or friend may be able to help.

TABLE 17-1 Ivy's OCD Worry Cycle for Checking OCD

Question	Answer
What are the specific situations or places that trigger my obsessions?	Whenever I leave my house or before bed, I have to check my door and window locks, and then check my security system, including my cameras, to make sure the house is secure. This happens again when I return home and then again before I go to bed. It takes me about 30 minutes on a good day to do the checking. But on bad days, I can get stuck for well over an hour.
What do I think will happen if I don't check?	I'm sure someone will break in and kill me and my family. If I'm not home, they'll wait for me to get home and then kill us.
How much distress do I feel? A little? A lot? A great deal?	I'm nervous and terrified most of the time. My family and coworkers think I'm nuts. And I'm always in trouble because my checking makes me late for work, and checking my phone to look at my security cameras annoys my boss. I'm also having a hard time keeping up with my work, and I end up taking it home to do in the evenings and on weekends.
What do I do to help myself with the distress? What do I avoid? What actions do I perform to protect myself and others?	I avoid going out at night. Not only do I have my checking routine at home, but at work I'm constantly looking at my phone. I watch the cameras that I have at both outside doors, over my garage, and in the backyard.
How much relief do I feel after avoiding or checking? For how long?	I feel compelled to do the checking, but I really don't get much relief from it. But if I didn't check, my anxiety would turn to panic, so I have no choice.

WORKSHEET 17-1 My OCD Worry Cycle

Question	Answer
What are the specific situations or places that trigger my obsessions?	
What do I think will happen if I don't check?	
How much distress do I feel? A little? A lot? A great deal?	
What do I do to help myself with the distress? What do I avoid? What actions do I perform to protect myself and others?	
How much relief do I feel after avoiding or checking? For how long?	

What are your reactions to seeing your worry cycle. Does it give you a better understanding about how OCD feeds on itself? Write your thoughts in Worksheet 17-2.

Preparing a list and rating the ugh factor

In Part 3, I describe ERP in detail. In this chapter, I zero in on developing a plan if you have doubting and checking OCD. You'll make a list of your OCD triggers and how anxious they make you feel. To give you an idea, here's Ivy's list. Ivy worries about keeping her house safe and compulsively checks her security system and locks.

WORKSHEET 17-2 **My Reflections on My OCD Worry Cycle**

Table 17-2 lists her triggers and how much distress she feels. She rates her distress with an ugh factor on a scale of 0 to 10, with 0 being no distress, 5 being moderate, and 10 being severe.

TABLE 17-2 **Ivy's Trigger List and Ugh Factor**

Trigger	Ugh Factor (0–10)
Not rechecking the locks and security system at least three times before I leave the house	8
Not checking the locks and security system at least three times before bed	10
Being in the car and not able to check my phone to see if the cameras are working	4
Being at work in a meeting where I can't check my phone	6 (or sometimes more if I start thinking about it)
Leaving the house in the evening	7

Ivy's trigger and ugh factors are the beginning steps to an ERP plan. She would likely begin by reducing her checking in the morning by at least one time (instead of doing so dozens of times) and possibly turning off her phone for periods of time throughout the day.

In Worksheet 17-3, make your own trigger list and rate the amount of distress you feel.

WORKSHEET 17-3 My Trigger List and Ugh Factor

Trigger	Ugh Factor (0–10)

Catching checking compulsions

Doubting and checking OCD involves compulsions that are attempts to either make sure something is okay or prevent a catastrophe. For example, someone may check their memory by going over some conversation they had to make sure they didn't say anything wrong or hurtful. Someone else may turn appliances on and off repeatedly to make sure that they're really off, hoping to prevent a fire.

Other people with checking compulsions scan the environment for possible dangers related to toxins. You can see that, like many forms of OCD, contamination and checking can be interrelated.

Someone with hit-and-run OCD repeatedly turns their car around to check and see if they ran someone over. This can involve getting out of the car to check the side of the road. They may drive off and then have that uncomfortable feeling again and once again return to the "scene."

When you experience that sense of doubt, what are your checking compulsions? Describe them in Worksheet 17-4.

Starting exposure and response prevention

ERP involves sitting with anxiety and fear until it decreases over time. This method is explained in detail in Part 3. The basic premise is to be exposed to your obsessions and then not complete your compulsive action. Generally, the compulsion is delayed at first and then gradually extinguished. This practice is repeated until the level of distress is decreased.

WORKSHEET 17-4 My Reflections on My Checking Compulsions

When you're doing exposures, you have to rely on quite a bit of self-discipline and self-control. There are many temptations and ways to sabotage your own treatment. It's important to be honest with yourself and your therapist. If you find something too difficult, there is no rush — step back and do something easier.

REMEMBER

If you find yourself having difficulty carrying out ERP on your own, please seek help from a mental health professional. Be honest about your struggles. It's perfectly normal to be challenged by doing exposures.

Are you working on ERP? How is it going for you? What have you learned about yourself? Reflect on these questions in Worksheet 17-5.

WORKSHEET 17-5 My Reflections on ERP

Dealing with Risks and Uncertainty

Many people with doubting and checking OCD don't seek treatment. They believe that they're acting in a responsible manner to manage risk and ensure safety. They respond with intense anxiety about the possible risk of not checking and rechecking.

This makes treating people with doubting obsessions and checking compulsions very difficult because there is no absolute certainty in life. Even when risks are relatively low, those with that extreme doubt have trouble believing that. Unfortunately, those who do seek treatment often drop out early and are highly resistant to treatment.

For those who have the need to be certain, the following may be helpful:

- Acknowledge that there is never 100 percent certainty.
- Embrace the idea that life is not predictable.
- Realize that thoughts or feelings are not necessarily accurate.

- Live in the present moment.
- Focus on getting through each day the best you can.

Do you have trouble with worry about uncertainty? Do you believe that you're responsible for keeping everyone safe? See if some of the preceding statements can help you live a more accepting life. Write your thoughts in Worksheet 17-6.

WORKSHEET 17-6 My Reflections on the Uncertainty of Life

Defeating and Correcting Distorted Thoughts

Distortions in thinking change the way you think and feel. Chapter 12 describes the most common cognitive distortions. For people with doubting and checking OCD, the following are typical distortions:

- **Emotional reasoning:** If I'm worried or frightened, there must be danger or trouble.
- **Catastrophizing:** If I don't stay vigilant, terrible things will happen and it will be my fault.
- **Dismissing evidence:** Just because it has never happened before and everyone thinks I'm safe doesn't mean it won't happen.

Do you find yourself using any of those distortions? Ask yourself if you're confusing your feelings with facts. Are there other ways to look at the situation? Is there evidence to support your conclusions? Is there any evidence against this thought? Write about your distortions in Worksheet 17-7.

WORKSHEET 17-7 My Reflections on My Distortions

Soothing Solutions

Working to combat doubting and checking OCD is challenging. Expect to have some distress. The good news is that with time and treatment, your discomfort will certainly decrease. During your treatment, be sure to identify some activities that you can do for yourself to give yourself a little love and pampering. Take some time to be self-compassionate.

Be sure to reward yourself for completing a difficult ERP session. Maybe some shopping therapy, a special night out, or a deep massage can be your reward. Recognize that you're working hard to feel better.

REMEMBER

You are not your OCD. Be proud. Give yourself a pat on the back.

Accepting and Moving Forward

Progress takes time. Expect peaks and valleys. Successful therapy doesn't eliminate all negative thoughts. Negative thoughts still provide you with information about what's happening. Hopefully, you've gained the skills to tell the difference between helpful, accurate thoughts and distorted thoughts.

REMEMBER

You can now accept that life is filled with uncertainty and understand that despite uncertainty, you have the power to live a life consistent with your deep, meaningful values.

IN THIS CHAPTER

» Keeping things too tidy

» Cluttering up the house

» Accepting and moving on

Chapter 18
Messing with Symmetry

Symmetry obsessive-compulsive disorder (OCD) involves an obsession about keeping or doing things in a particular, "correct" way. That correct way feels "just right." If something feels unbalanced, incomplete, or somehow off, the person with symmetry OCD feels great tension. Whether it's folding clothes in a particular way or arranging books on bookshelves by color, shape, or size, when something is out of order, the person experiences considerable distress. A person with symmetry OCD may feel a compulsive need to turn lights on and off a certain number of times or park their car in a specific spot.

Those with these obsessions and compulsions often feel that the time spent on keeping things in order is perfectly reasonable and necessary. That makes this type of OCD difficult to change. Treatment is often sought after multiple complaints from family members who are expected to keep up with or put up with unrealistic demands.

In this chapter, I present a treatment plan for those with ordering or symmetry OCD.

Messing Things Up

Sometimes called "just right" OCD, symptoms are extremely diverse. Some common examples include arranging items such as books, cupboards, or clothing in a particular way. Other symptoms involve straightening the pictures on the wall, the fringe on a carpet, the pillows on a couch, objects around the house, or furniture.

Symmetry can also involve a need for evening up. Actions such as walking through a doorway need to be done in a certain prescribed way or they must be repeated. Touching, tapping, and counting are also done in particular ways. If balance is not achieved, people with symmetry OCD feel overwhelming distress and fear that something bad may happen.

Exposure and response prevention (ERP) is the best evidence-based treatment for this type of OCD. The following sections show you how to design your own ERP plan. For more information on ERP, see Part 3.

TIP

If your OCD is significantly interfering with your everyday life, I strongly recommend that you work with a therapist trained in ERP.

Understanding the worry cycle for symmetry OCD

People with symmetry OCD become anxious when they perceive that things are out of balance or order. Then they feel compelled to make things right and feel a sense of temporary relief. However, that relief is short-lived and obsessions return. That's their OCD worry cycle.

In this section, you can map out your own worry cycle. The following example shows you how Liam is caught in a vicious circle of obsessions and compulsions. Liam wakes up each morning and sits up in bed. He must place both feet on the floor at the same time. If one of his feet touches first or if the pressure of his feet on the floor feels different to him, he must lie back down in bed and try again to achieve the proper balance. He gets frustrated when things don't feel right and often spends 10 or 15 minutes just getting out of bed. Thus, his day of obsessive thoughts about needing balance and symmetry begins. The description of his OCD cycle in Table 18-1 illustrates his distress.

TABLE 18-1 Liam's OCD Cycle for Symmetry OCD

Question	Answer
What are the specific situations or places that trigger my obsessions?	I obsess about balance and movement. When I move positions from one place to another, my feet need to work at the same speed and have the same amount of pressure. This happens throughout the day whenever I'm walking or standing. I'm also extremely organized. I have to have everything in my house arranged in the perfect way.
What do I think will happen if I don't have balance?	I don't know exactly what will happen, but certainly something awful. It seems dangerous to me.
How much distress do I feel? A little? A lot? A great deal?	I'm agonizing about this from the moment I wake up until I fall asleep. My stress level is out of this world. Every step I take must be calculated. I'm constantly rearranging things at home so that they're just right.
What do I do to help myself with the distress? What do I avoid? What actions do I perform to protect myself and others?	I have to repeat steps constantly until they're balanced. I'm almost always late for appointments because of the repeating. When I'm not obsessing about my steps, I'm arranging things at home. I avoid going anywhere that I don't have to go.
How much relief do I feel after I get the correct balance? For how long?	I get a moment of relief when my steps are balanced, but when I have to move again, the tension returns. And as soon as I organize something, I get the feeling that something is off, so I have to reorganize.

Liam leads a small, tortured life. He is constantly worried about moving and order and wastes much of his day on obsessively worrying and compulsively repeating steps or organizing cupboards. His slowness has impacted all areas of his life.

Describe your own OCD cycle in Worksheet 18-1. You can fill out this worksheet by yourself or with your therapist. If you have a trusted close friend or family member, share it with them and ask for feedback.

WORKSHEET 18-1 My OCD Worry Cycle

Question	Answer
What are the specific situations or places that trigger my obsessions?	
What do I think will happen if I don't have balance?	
How much distress do I feel? A little? A lot? A great deal?	
What do I do to help myself with the distress? What do I avoid? What actions do I perform to protect myself and others?	
How much relief do I feel after I get the correct balance? For how long?	

After completing this exercise, take a few minutes to experience your feelings in Worksheet 18-2. What are your reactions to seeing your worry cycle? Does it give you a better understanding of how OCD feeds on itself?

WORKSHEET 18-2 My Reflections on My OCD Worry Cycle

Preparing a list and rating the ugh factor

When you understand your own OCD worry cycle, you can develop a list of triggers and the amount of distress each trigger causes.

REMEMBER

In order to choose what issues you'll work on, you need to rate the amount of distress you feel when you're faced with a trigger. The ugh factor is a scale of 0 to 10, used to measure distress, with 0 being no distress at all, 5 being moderate, and 10 being extremely anxious and disturbed.

Liam, in the earlier example, has an obsessive need for balance. As a result, he spends huge amounts of time making things feel just so. To help you make your own trigger list, Table 18-2 shows an example of Liam's.

TABLE 18-2 Liam's Trigger List and Ugh Factor Rating

Trigger	Ugh Factor (0–10)
Feeling that my steps are not even	9
Forgetting how many steps I've taken	6
Obsessing about my cupboards	8
Getting out of bed without putting both feet down in the same way and at the same time	10
Walking through doorways in public places	5
Seeing that my closet is not perfectly arranged	9

Now, you make your own trigger list and rate the ugh factor for your contamination obsessions in Worksheet 18-3.

WORKSHEET 18-3 My Trigger List and Ugh Factor Rating

Trigger	Ugh Factor (0–10)

Capturing compulsions

Ordering and symmetry OCD typically involve compulsive actions to achieve that "just right" feeling. They often include:

- Arranging items in a particular way
- Making sure that items in the home or office are even or balanced

- Walking in a certain way
- Evening up (for example, if one side of the body does something, the other side must do the same thing)
- Redoing things such as writing, cleaning, or folding until they feel right
- Counting, chanting, tapping, or speaking in a special way
- Having to repeat putting something away in a precise pattern
- Washing or showering in a particular balanced or prescribed way (not because of contamination concerns)

REMEMBER

Everyone with OCD is unique. Your symptoms may not always fit into any certain category. And many of these compulsions and obsessions overlap and change.

In Worksheet 18-4, take some time to think about and write down the compulsions you engage in following your obsession for symmetry, order, or being just right.

WORKSHEET 18-4 My Reflections

Starting exposure and response prevention

Now you have the information you need to develop your own ERP treatment. You understand the OCD worry cycle, and you've identified the triggers and the compulsions that follow.

Choose a few triggers and set up an exposure session. If you're working with a therapist, share with them the work you've been doing in this chapter.

Let's return to the example of Liam who had a lot of problems with placing his feet in a certain order and with a certain amount of pressure. If I were working with Liam, I might have him start with placing his feet on the floor one at a time. He would stomp one foot but not the other. We'd have a timer and let him sit with his discomfort for maybe five minutes.

When his level of distress decreased, I would have him repeat the exposures multiple times. This would start the relearning process, proving that nothing horrible happens when his feet don't have the same amount of pressure.

This is hard work. It takes patience and time. For more strategies and details see Part 3.

Straightening Out Distorted Thoughts

People with ordering or symmetry OCD believe that something awful may happen if they don't make sure that things are just right. Common cognitive distortions (see Chapter 12) include:

- **Black-and-white thinking:** If things aren't exactly right, they're horrible.
- **Dismissing evidence:** Nothing has happened when things get out of order or balance, but something possibly could.
- **Emotional reasoning:** I feel uncomfortable when something isn't right, so it must mean that something bad will happen if I don't fix, straighten, or correct it.
- **Thought/action fusion:** I think something is off so it must be. I need to fix it.

Identify your distorted thoughts. You may try to check the evidence to see whether your thoughts are realistic. Answer the following questions:

- What evidence do I have that supports this thought?
- Is there any evidence that refutes this thought?
- Is this thought illogical or distorted in any way?
- Is this thought based on how I feel, or is it based on fact?
- Have I ever tested out this thought?
- Are there any times in my life that this thought wouldn't be true?
- How horrible would the consequences be of giving up this thought?
- Is this thought helping me lead a better life?

In Worksheet 18-5, reflect on your answers to these questions here. Can you come up with any more adaptable thoughts?

WORKSHEET 18-5 My Reflections on My Distorted Thoughts

Soothing Solutions

Treatment for OCD requires sitting with some amount of distress. This is challenging both emotionally and physically. It's important during treatment to take good care of your body and mind. Make sure that you're getting adequate sleep, eat a healthy diet, and be sure to exercise.

When you're stressed, choose a few methods that work for you to wind down. Breathing or meditation practices work wonders for anxiety and stress. Listening to music or a favorite podcast can help you relax. Be sure to stay connected to friends and family.

Find some special ways to reward yourself for getting through ERP. Have a piece of chocolate or arrange a massage. Make a date with a friend for lunch or treat yourself to a movie. Good job!

Accepting and Moving Forward

When you die, do you want your obituary to read:

- The clothes in the closet were arranged by color, and each hanger was ½ inch from the next.
- The fringe in the living room was perfectly groomed.
- They made sure that everything stayed in the correct spot.
- Their canned goods were arranged in alphabetical order.
- They were known to have special rituals that they repeated in a certain way.

Of course you don't. You want someone to mention your accomplishments, your family, your friends. Or possibly your kindness to others, your participation in some cause, or your dedication to your friends and colleagues.

Realize that OCD takes you away from your values. What are the important qualities that you want to be remembered for? Think about those, accept your OCD symptoms, and move forward. Live the life you want to have.

IN THIS CHAPTER

» Listening to upsetting chatter

» Understanding that thoughts don't mean actions

» Looking at ways to overcome revolving thoughts

Chapter 19

Responding to Revolving Thoughts

When most people think about obsessive-compulsive disorder (OCD), they think about checking the locks, repeatedly washing hands, or strange rituals. These are all compulsions related to obsessional thoughts. However, many people with OCD primarily have obsessive thoughts without frequent or obvious compulsions.

These obsessive thoughts are most often filled with immoral, disgusting, inappropriate, and horrible behaviors, impulses, or images. They often include images of sexually inappropriate, morally disgusting, or violent behavior. And sometimes these obsessions are accompanied with strong impulses to act out these thoughts. However, it's important to know that people with this type of OCD hardly ever act out these thoughts (I'd say never, but that's impossible to prove).

Unfortunately, those with these shame-filled thoughts often suffer in silence. They are too embarrassed to tell anyone. They may have some compulsive responses such as praying or other mental rituals. However, they live in a secret hell, rarely asking for help.

REMEMBER

Everyone has weird thoughts from time to time. Some are disgusting and unwanted. That's perfectly normal. It's when the thoughts keep coming and interfere with your life and well-being that it becomes a problem.

This chapter presents some strategies and ideas specific to primarily obsessional OCD. Many of these strategies are explained in more detail throughout the chapters of this book.

Existential Angst: Shame and Guilt

People with this type of OCD usually have thoughts that center around a theme of not being able to stay in control. Some examples include:

- Becoming violent or hurting someone
- Fear of saying something inappropriate, such as swearing
- Thoughts about sexually acting out
- Thoughts that they may soil themselves
- Worry that they may vomit in public
- Questioning their sexual identity
- Viewing themselves as sinners or blasphemous

Although people with these obsessions don't act them out, they worry all the time that once, just once, they may lose all self-control and do the horrible thing that they're thinking about.

The next sections help you develop an exposure and response prevention (ERP) strategy to try. Part 3 of this book describes these techniques in detail.

REMEMBER

ERP is the gold standard treatment for OCD.

Understanding the OCD worry cycle

People who obsessively worry about doing something shameful or losing control are stuck in a cycle of worry and catastrophe. In this section, you have the opportunity to complete the worry cycle so you can better understand the loop you're participating in.

WARNING

The thoughts of those with primarily obsessive OCD are often quite shocking. There may be gruesome images, strange sexual behaviors, or grossly immoral thoughts. People who think these things are struggling, but they aren't terrible people at all.

To help you fill out your own worry cycle, Table 19-1 offers an example of Charlie, a twenty-something who worries that he might attack and sexually abuse dogs. Charlie has shame-based OCD. He doesn't actually become physically aroused around dogs, but he has constant thoughts that he may suddenly lose control and try to have sex with dogs.

Charlie is depressed and possibly suicidal because of his uncontrollable, sexually deviant thoughts. Charlie is a good person who has never been in any sort of trouble because of sexual deviancy. These thoughts came out of nowhere and plague Charlie without mercy. The thoughts interfere with his life and take up considerable time each day. Charlie gets little relief from praying.

TABLE 19-1 Charlie's OCD Cycle

Question	Answer
What are the specific situations or places that trigger my obsessions?	Almost everywhere I go, there are small dogs. I have constant thoughts when I see them. It's so weird. I also have these thoughts randomly throughout the day. I hate having these thoughts.
What do I think will happen if I keep having these thoughts?	One day I'm going to crack up and just try to hump a dog. I can't believe I said that, but that's what I imagine I might do.
How much distress do I feel? A little? A lot? A great deal?	I'm a ridiculous, horrible person. I feel like some sort of pervert. I don't understand what's wrong with me. Honestly, sometimes I feel like I should just be gone from this world.
What do I do to help myself with the distress? What do I avoid? What actions do I take to protect myself and others?	If I can avoid seeing a dog, I will. And when I start having these thoughts I try to pray to God to help me. I know I'm probably going to hell, but maybe God will save me. I repeat the same prayers asking for forgiveness, and sometimes that gets rid of the thoughts.
How much relief do I feel after I perform a mental ritual? For how long?	A bit. I get some hope, but never for long. The thoughts keep on coming back regardless of what I do. I'm such a creep.

Now it's time to describe your own OCD cycle in Worksheet 19-1. Take your time and thoughtfully complete the worksheet. You can fill this out by yourself or with your therapist. If you have a trusted close friend or family member, share it with them and ask for feedback.

WORKSHEET 19-1 My OCD Cycle

Question	Answer
What are the specific situations or places that trigger my obsessions?	
What do I think will happen if I keep having these thoughts?	
How much distress do I feel? A little? A lot? A great deal?	
What do I do to help myself with the distress? What do I avoid? What actions do I take to protect myself and others?	
How much relief do I feel after I perform a mental ritual? For how long?	

What are your reactions to seeing your OCD cycle? Does it give you a better understanding about how OCD feeds on itself? Write your thoughts in Worksheet 19-2.

Preparing a list and rating the ugh factor

The next step in developing an ERP plan is to identify specific triggers that seem to increase your obsessive thinking. Then rate the amount of distress using a 1-to-10 scale, where 1 means little or no distress, 5 means a moderate level of distress, and 10 means horrible distress.

WORKSHEET 19-2 My Reflections on My OCD Cycle

If I happened to be working with Charlie, I might help him develop the trigger list in Table 19-2. Then Charlie would indicate the level of distress.

TABLE 19-2 Charlie's Trigger List and Ugh Factor Rating

Trigger	Ugh Factor (0–10)
Hearing other people talk about dogs	6
Going for a walk and being near dogs	10
Not doing anything	4
Seeing pictures of dogs	5
Writing down my creepy thoughts	8
Telling my therapist my thoughts	10

TIP

Many people with shame-based or primarily obsessional OCD need help from a trained therapist to develop a treatment plan to address their symptoms. I encourage most people with OCD to consider psychotherapy.

Now, make your own trigger list and rate the ugh factor for your obsessive thoughts in Worksheet 19-3. Don't forget, if you need help, a therapist won't be shocked or judge you for your thoughts.

WORKSHEET 19-3 My Trigger List and Ugh Factor Rating

Trigger	Ugh Factor (0–10)

Contemplating compulsions

The compulsions of people with primarily obsessional OCD are usually covert. That means they're usually mental acts that can't be seen or noticed by other people. These usually include attempts to:

- Suppress the thought
- Change the thought
- Do a mental ritual to "undo" the thought
- Neutralize the thought with a different thought
- Pray away the thought

These strategies simply don't work. Even if you experience a brief respite, you can be sure the thoughts will come roaring back.

Starting exposure and response prevention

For those with contamination OCD, ERP training involves getting in the dirt. But with shame-based OCD, you obviously can't engage in the feared activity. For example, someone with the fear of losing control of their bodily functions isn't expected to urinate in public.

For this reason, much of the work involves *imagined* exposure rather than *actual* exposure. An exposure may be imagining yourself urinating on a busy street. Exposures also involve speaking out loud about the feared obsession, as well as writing them down multiple times.

Another way to expose yourself to horrific thoughts is to make an audio recording on your phone. For instance, if you fear hurting someone impulsively, you might record, "I obsessively worry that I may lose control and start strangling a stranger. I see someone right now that may be my first victim. I may not be able to stop myself. I'm a monster."

Listen to that a hundred times, and it'll eventually become boring. You may consider wearing ear pods and listening to the recording on your phone while you go about your day.

What is your own plan for ERP? Describe it in Worksheet 19-4. If you're having any trouble, get professional help.

WORKSHEET 19-4 My Plan for ERP

Defining and Defeating Distorted Thoughts

Thought distortions are habitual ways of thinking that ignore evidence and exaggerate or misrepresent reality. They shape the way you interpret the world around you. See Chapter 12 for more information and examples of how thought distortions work. Here are some common distortions relevant to shame-based primarily obsessive OCD:

- **Thought-action fusion:** Believing that if you think something bad, it reflects on you. This is the primary distortion at work behind shame-based OCD. You may have a strong belief that if you think about doing something violent, horrible, sexually perverted, or blasphemous, you must be a terrible person.

» **Emotional reasoning:** Believing that negative feelings are accurate representations of reality. Those who think of themselves as unworthy human beings tend to feel bad, which kicks in emotional reasoning, in which your negative feelings about yourself confirm that you must truly *be* a bad person.

» **Dismissing the evidence:** Maintaining a negative interpretation despite evidence that disputes the accuracy of that belief. Your beliefs that you're a bad person are encouraged because you dismiss the evidence that you've never acted on these beliefs and fear that someday you'll lose control and act out your thoughts.

» **Mind reading:** Believing that you absolutely know what other people are thinking. Most people with primarily obsessional OCD believe that other people must know that they're horrible. They assume that they can read the minds of others.

All these distortions lead to an increase of strong feelings of unworthiness.

Do you find yourself using any of these thought distortions? If you do, are you confusing thoughts with actions or feelings with facts? Are you dismissing any evidence or attempting to read the minds of others? Are there other ways of looking at your obsessional thinking? Reflect on those in Worksheet 19-5.

WORKSHEET 19-5 My Reflections on My Thought Distortions

Soothing Solutions

While you're treating your OCD, you're likely to experience an increase in distress. The good news is that with treatment, the increase is only temporary. So, it's important that during treatment you give yourself a lot of compassion. Here are some ways to do that:

- Plan some time for relaxation.
- Eat well.
- Get enough sleep.
- Practice deep breathing.
- Engage in regular exercise.
- Get out and socialize with friends or family.
- Don't judge yourself — you're doing the best you can.
- Give yourself a big hug.

Moving Forward with Acceptance

You've struggled with OCD. Acknowledge the distress you feel. Realize that you've survived so far and you can get better. Focus on what's in front of you now:

- What do you see?
- What do you hear?
- What do you smell?
- What can you feel?

Sit with the distress. It will pass. Thoughts and feelings come and go. Take stock of your values and go forward with your life.

7
The Part of Tens

IN THIS PART . . .

Look for and respond to relapse.

Manage and reduce stress.

IN THIS CHAPTER

» Knowing all about relapses

» Figuring out your odds

» Challenging your negative thoughts

Chapter 20

Ten (or So) Ways to Respond to Relapse

Most people with obsessive-compulsive disorder (OCD) don't actually have a complete recovery, in which all symptoms are eliminated forever. You may experience *lapses*, brief episodes of mild symptoms that tend to be short-lived. Lapses are common when you experience loss, when your life is overly demanding, or when you're sick or tired. When your life gets back to normal, your symptoms will likely decrease.

A *relapse*, on the other hand, starts out gradually, but the symptoms grow and become overwhelming. A relapse should be taken seriously. This chapter offers more information on relapses and strategies for dealing with them.

WARNING

Relapse rates are quite high for those who take medication for OCD and stop taking their meds. Over three-quarters of those who stop taking their medication will experience a relapse. The opposite is true for those who complete exposure and response prevention (ERP) therapy — about three-quarters of those people tend to maintain the gains in symptom reduction that they achieved in therapy.

In this chapter, I paint a realistic picture of the rates of relapse and provide some tips, tricks, and techniques to deal with the, hopefully, small bumps in the road.

Don't Catastrophize

It's natural to start imagining the worst when you experience a relapse of OCD. Your brain may naturally start spiraling, thinking you're back at square one. But the problem with getting overly upset when you have a return of OCD is that emotional distress only adds fuel to the fire. Your distress makes your symptoms surge.

REMEMBER

You were able to battle through your OCD before. You had a period of time when you were pretty much okay. If you were able to do it once, you're likely to get back to where you were before your relapse — and it won't be as hard because you've been here before.

You can handle this temporary setback and possibly grow from it, which will make you even stronger and better prepared the next time.

Be Aware of Your Slips in Thinking

If you absolutely can't stand to have OCD symptoms, they'll surely appear. Having a bit of OCD is not the end of the world. If your relapse is making you totally miserable, put it into perspective. Many talented, successful people lead meaningful, full lives despite their OCD.

You've built resilience during treatment. You'll be able to manage a relapse now just as you were able to manage your OCD before.

Identify Triggers

OCD relapses often appear when someone is experiencing stress. Interestingly, not all stressful events are negative — both positive and negative events can cause stress and increase your risk of relapses. The following events could potentially lead to a relapse:

- Suffering an illness, whether short-term or long-term
- Losing an important relationship
- Experiencing financial stress (for example, losing your job)
- Not getting enough sleep or not sleeping well
- Feeling overworked
- Being rejected or criticized
- Graduating from school
- Getting married
- Having a baby
- Retiring

» Getting a new job

» Moving

TIP

Not all stressful events result in a relapse. And relapses don't have to lead to a complete return of symptoms.

Do What Worked Before

If you're reading this chapter, you likely had treatment for your OCD and got significantly better. Now your symptoms have returned. Try a few of the techniques that helped you before and see if they help.

If you took medicine and stopped taking it, you may want to contact your medical provider and start up again. If you did ERP, do a few exposures on your own. If cognitive therapy worked for you, start keeping track of your thoughts — perhaps you're having thought distortions. If acceptance and mindfulness worked for you, start up a new practice.

Give it a try for a week or so and see if your symptoms resolve or decrease. Tell yourself that you recovered before and you can do it again. If your symptoms don't resolve or decrease, check out the next section.

Do Something Different

If you try what worked before and that just isn't helping, take another route. If you took medication, try psychotherapy with a therapist who has knowledge of and experience working with clients who have OCD.

If you achieved good results with psychotherapy and you've attempted some techniques on your own, you may want to consider medication.

TIP

Take a look at Parts 3, 4, and 5 of this book for more strategies for addressing OCD symptoms.

Check Whether You're Using Emotional Reasoning

Emotional reasoning occurs when you feel something, such as anxiety, and conclude that if you're anxious, there must actually be something scary around, or if you feel guilty or embarrassed, you've done something shameful or wrong.

In other words, you believe your feelings are evidence of danger or wrongdoing. When you trust your feelings to be accurate reflections of reality, your risk of relapse is great. So, if you have contamination OCD, your *feeling* is one of unease and you wash your hands one more time. If you have shame-based OCD, you feel compelled to pray or repent for a *feeling* not for something you really did.

If you have an occasional negative feeling that leads to an obsessive thought, impulse, or image, that's normal. And if you infrequently give up and act compulsively, it's not that big of a deal. But it can be a slippery slope — a lapse can easily become a relapse. Check the evidence.

REMEMBER

Emotions and feelings are signals that give you information. But these signals aren't always true. Just because you *feel* something doesn't make it true.

Accept Negative Feelings

Negative feelings are part of living. Feelings come in pairs. You can't know what happy is if you've never been sad. You can't know what relaxed feels like if you've never been anxious. It's important to understand that having a negative feeling is perfectly normal.

TIP

Don't fight your feelings. Accept them. Observe them. Watch them come and go in waves of intensity. Stand back and notice that they're temporary. Stay with discomfort, but don't engage in compulsive behavior. You're strong and you can handle a bit of distress. Now, move forward with your life.

Remain Vigilant

In all likelihood, you'll have occasional symptoms of OCD. Pay attention to high-risk situations that may trigger your symptoms. Prepare for them by making a plan to keep your stress low and have some strategies ready when symptoms return. Use self-soothing strategies such as deep breathing or meditation (see Chapter 13).

TIP

Consider keeping a log of symptoms. Monitoring symptoms is a great way to gather information that helps you determine if your OCD is mild or getting more prevalent. Just don't obsess about monitoring or get compulsive about making sure that your log is just right. You don't need to do it every day. And if, after some time, you find that monitoring isn't helpful, stop.

Consider a Tune-Up with a Professional

If your relapse is interfering with your life, you've given some self-help strategies a try, and your symptoms remain, find some professional support. Admitting you have a problem is sometimes difficult. But ignoring it will likely lead to an increase in symptoms.

REMEMBER

By getting professional help, you're showing your strength, not your weakness. It takes courage to show up and work on your problems. A few booster sessions may be all you need.

IN THIS CHAPTER

» Taking deep breaths

» Moving through OCD

» Living a meaningful life

Chapter 21

Ten Strategies to Reduce Stress

A big part of the treatment of obsessive-compulsive disorder (OCD) is accepting and feeling distress. However, sometimes you just need a break from negative feelings. The following ideas can help you calm down and even distract yourself.

WARNING

Use the following ideas for quick, temporary relief from OCD. Used too often, however, these techniques can become ways to avoid facing the discomfort you need to feel to get better. They can even turn into rituals that become compulsions.

Practice Breathing for Relaxation

The best part of building a breathing exercise routine is that you can do it anywhere. You don't need to make a lot of noise, carry any equipment, or be obvious when you're practicing your breathing. And you have to breathe anyway, so you may as well get some added benefit.

You can choose among many different patterns of breathing (see Chapter 12 for many examples). The majority of these breathing patterns can be discreetly done in any setting. Choose a couple that don't involve loud hissing to have handy when you're stressed out.

The most important components to all breathing exercises are:

- Slowing down your breathing
- Breathing deeply
- Concentrating on your breathing

Exercise More

If you're having an obsession or feeling distressed, there is no quicker technique than exercise. Stop what you're doing and do some push-ups or jumping jacks or anything that works your body. I guarantee that negative thinking isn't compatible with vigorous exercise. Get moving as fast as you can, and you'll get out of breath and feel better.

Regular exercise is a critical component of leading a healthy life. It can also be a quick fix for anxiety or distress.

TIP

Even most people with disabilities or frailty can benefit from movement. Consult with your doctor or physical therapist before starting an exercise program appropriate for you.

WARNING

People with OCD can be a bit, well, obsessive. They can easily start doing exercise as a way of coping, and exercise can become a compulsion. Don't neglect treatment for OCD because you think exercise is a cure. It's simply a strategy for reducing distress in the present moment. It doesn't replace treatment.

Step Away from OCD

When you're having symptoms, imagine yourself sitting on top of a cloud. You're looking down at your OCD from far away. You aren't OCD. OCD is something that is a small part of you, but it isn't the essence of who you are.

Observe your obsessions and compulsions as actions and impulses. They're drifting away. You're separate and distinct.

Distract

Distraction involves turning your attention into either a mentally or physically stimulating activity. This activity is a personal choice. It could be reading, art, or a challenging puzzle. Before engaging in distraction, it's good to check in with your feelings. Then mindfully engage in the valued activity.

Make a List of Affirmations

Use your notes app on your phone and write out some statements that can help you keep a balanced perspective. Sometimes when anxiety levels are high, it's hard to think rationally. Having a few affirmations in your phone when you need a reminder can be helpful. Here are a few ideas, but feel free to make your own:

- Just because I feel anxious, it doesn't mean there is danger.
- I feel guilty, but I did nothing wrong.
- Thoughts are just thoughts. They aren't always true.
- Having weird thoughts doesn't make me a terrible person.
- Feelings come and go. They increase and decrease.
- I am able to handle this. I've done so in the past.

Read through your list when you feel overwhelmed and see if they help. Add to your list when you learn new things through your own self-help endeavors or through therapy.

Sleep Stories

Good sleep is important for overall health. Sleep promotes brain function, improves memory, and restores the body. Sleep, for people with OCD, can frequently be interrupted by intrusive thoughts. I don't recommend getting up in the middle of the night and performing exposure and response prevention (ERP).

Sleep stories are calm, relaxing narrations that are written and spoken in gentle language. They're designed to capture your racing thoughts and calm your brain. They lack plots, strong language, and upsetting subjects. They're just interesting enough to focus on, but they lack a compelling reason to finish the story. Most sleep stories involve sensory experiences such as the warmth from a campfire, the beauty of a garden, or soft comfortable places.

You can find sleep stories on meditation apps. Some are narrated by celebrities. Almost all apps have free trial subscriptions, so try one out a night or two. You may feel surprisingly sleepy.

Go Outside

Being outside for less than 30 minutes can improve your physical and mental health. It reduces the levels of stress hormones that have a negative impact on your health. In addition, being outside improves:

- Concentration and focus
- Problem-solving

» Creativity
» Sleep
» Energy
» Mood

You don't need to go for a run, although doing so would be an added bonus. You can just sit outside and breathe, enjoy the sounds of nature, and take in the sights. A daily walk is a wonderful way to get both exercise and the benefits of being outside. You don't need to have woods nearby — try to find a place with some grass, plants, or trees such as a park, your neighborhood, your own patio, or backyard.

Socialize

People with OCD often withdraw from others because of either fear or shame. Loneliness is a risk factor for cardiovascular disease, type 2 diabetes, increased depression, higher levels of anxiety, dementia, and an early death. So, it's critical for everyone to have a social support system.

Socializing reduces stress, improves cognitive function, and decreases loneliness. Having a few close friends is more important than having a large social circle. For those with OCD, having a social life can actually be a form of exposure to feared social judgment or shame. It can also be an opportunity for friends to be understanding and supportive, which can encourage more treatment.

Volunteer

Volunteering is one of the best ways of meeting new people and increasing meaning and purpose in your life. If you're too shy, make it an opportunity to take a chance. There are many opportunities, from handing out food at a food bank to tutoring children to restocking books at your local library. If you aren't much of a people person, volunteer at a local animal shelter. Shelters always need cat cuddlers and dog walkers.

You can research local opportunities by searching for "volunteer opportunities near me."

Start a Gratitude Practice

Multiple studies confirm that the act of practicing gratitude reduces stress, leads to better sleep, and improves both mental and physical health. A gratitude practice can include daily journaling or simply focusing on and noticing the positive moments of your life. Be grateful that you have the ability to think, reason, read, enjoy, move, breathe, eat, and drink.

How wonderful that you have enough to eat, a roof over your head, and drinking water. Be grateful for your friends, family, and acquaintances. Appreciate the warmth of the sun, a gentle breeze, or spring showers.

TIP

For those with OCD, it's important to not have gratitude become a compulsion. If you miss a day or even a week, just return to it here and there. And don't forget to be grateful for the progress you've made in your journey to overcome OCD.

Index

Numeric

A

B

C

F

About the Author

Laura L. Smith, PhD, is a clinical psychologist and a past president of the New Mexico Psychological Association. She has considerable experience in school, hospital, and clinical settings dealing with children, adolescents, and adults with obsessive-compulsive disorder, anxiety, depression, anger, and personality disorders.

Laura completed specialized training and was certified by the Behavior Training Institute of the International OCD Foundation. She was one of few psychologists in New Mexico with that specialized training and saw clients from across the state.

She has presented workshops on cognitive therapy and mental health issues to national and international audiences. She wrote *100 Questions & Answers About Anxiety For Dummies; 100 Questions & Answers About Depression For Dummies; 100 Questions & Answers About Borderline Personality Disorder For Dummies; Anxiety & Depression Workbook For Dummies*, 2nd Edition; *Anger Management For Dummies*, 3rd Edition; and *OCD For Dummies*, 2nd Edition (all published by Wiley).

Previously, Laura worked on numerous publications together with her husband, the late Charles Elliott, PhD. They were coauthors of *Anxiety For Dummies*, 3rd Edition; *Depression For Dummies*, 2nd Edition; *Quitting Smoking & Vaping For Dummies; Borderline Personality Disorder For Dummies*, 2nd Edition; *Child Psychology & Development For Dummies;* and *Seasonal Affective Disorder For Dummies* (all published by Wiley).

Dedication

To my kids and their partners, thank you for helping me get through major life transitions. I wouldn't be able to move forward without your strong support.

Author's Acknowledgments

First, I'd like to thank the wonderful team at Wiley who've supported my work through many projects. Acquisitions Editor Elizabeth Stilwell launched the idea of a workbook for OCD. Joe Bush, PhD, my technical editor, made sure the facts were straight. I want to especially thank Elizabeth Kuball, an editor extraordinaire — we've worked on several projects together and her editorial corrections and comments are always appreciated and spot on.

Publisher's Acknowledgments

Associate Editor: Elizabeth Stilwell
Senior Managing Editor: Kristie Pyles
Editor: Elizabeth Kuball
Technical Editor: Joseph P. Bush, PhD
Production Editor: Athiyappan Lalith Kumar
Cover Image: Nobilis Bellator/Getty Images
Special Help: Carmen Krikorian